FLY TYER'S GUIDE TO
TYING ESSENTIAL TROUT FLIES

FLY TYER'S GUIDE TO
TYING ESSENTIAL TROUT FLIES

David Klausmeyer

LYONS PRESS
An imprint of Globe Pequot Press
Guilford, Connecticut

Lyons Press is an imprint of Globe Pequot Press.

All interior photos by David Klausmeyer unless noted otherwise.

Project editor: Staci Zacharski
Text design and layout: Sue Murray

Library of Congress Cataloging-in-Publication Data

Klausmeyer, David, 1958-
  Fly tyer's guide to tying essential trout flies / Dave Klausmeyer.
     pages cm
  ISBN 978-0-7627-8751-7
1. Fly tying—Handbooks, manuals, etc. 2. Flies, Artificial. 3. Streamers (Fly fishing) 4. Trout fishing. I. Title. II. Title: Guide to tying essential trout flies.
  SH451.K5297 2013
  688.7'9124—dc23

                                                                              2013023722

Printed in the United States of America

10 9 8 7 6 5 4 3 2 1

CONTENTS

Chapter 1

Tooling Up

WHAT GEAR YOU NEED TO START TYING FLIES, AND WHAT YOU MIGHT WANT TO ADD TO YOUR BENCH AS YOU GAIN EXPERIENCE

Like any hobby, you'll need to acquire some tools to tie flies. And as with most activities, a fool can be quickly parted from his hard-earned money. This is especially true when selecting unfamiliar tools for a craft in which you have no experience: what do you absolutely need, what don't you need or can purchase later, what are considered reasonable prices, and what are the best brands? These are very reasonable questions, and there are some reasonable answers.

First, we'll discuss what you will need if you have never tied flies before; our goal is to select quality tools that will not break your bank account. Next, we'll examine a few items that you can add to your tool kit as you gain experience tying flies; these will add enjoyment to your time at the fly-tying bench or let you experiment with new ways of tying flies.

SELECTING YOUR FIRST VISE

The vise will be the centerpiece of your fly-tying station. Whether you create a permanent place in your home to tie flies, or you get out your tools and materials every time you sit down to tie, all the action will occur around your vise.

A vise has five basic components. First, the *jaws* grasp the hook while tying the fly. Second, the *locking mechanism* opens and closes the jaws. Third, the *head* of the vise holds both the jaws and locking

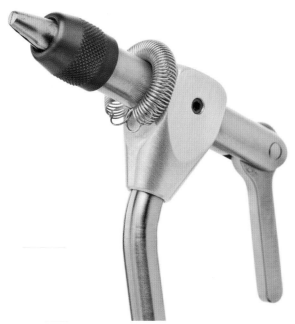

This is the head of a Dyna-King vise.

mechanism. Fourth, a *post* holds the head (and thus the jaws and locking mechanism) above the bench top. And fifth, you'll place the vise on your bench using a *clamp* or *pedestal base*. We'll consider each of these components in turn.

A vise must hold a hook securely; this is obvious. Nothing is more frustrating than having the hook move while tying a fly. All quality vises have jaws made of either high-carbon or stainless steel. Some jaws have smooth surfaces that hold the hook, while others have slight serrations that are supposed to help the jaws grasp the hook. Frankly, however, I have vises with smooth jaws that do a fine job of grasping hooks, and other vises with serrated jaws that do a mediocre job of holding hooks. Whether a vise has serrated jaws should play a minor role in your decision when making a purchase.

A more important consideration is whether the jaws can accommodate a wide range of hook sizes. The jaws on some vises readily handle everything from the smallest midge hooks to large saltwater irons; the jaws on other specialized vises are designed to accommodate, for example, very small hooks or magnum-size bass bug or saltwater hooks. If you know you will concentrate on tying bass or saltwater flies, you might prefer one of these specialized vises, or you might consider a vise that will allow you to change jaws. I prefer one vise that can do it all, and there are many options from which to choose.

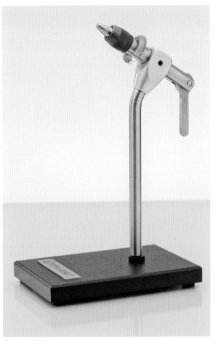

Dyna-King

There are several different styles of jaw-locking mechanisms, but we don't have to get into the specifics about these. What does it matter how a vise closes the jaws to grasp the hook? We simply want the vise to hold the hook firmly while tying the fly. I do not want, however, a vise that requires placing a lot of force on the locking mechanism to close the jaws tightly on the hook; undue force can crush and weaken the hook or fatigue some part of the vise.

I also prefer a vise that requires minimum adjustment of the locking mechanism when changing hook sizes; I want to spend my time tying flies, not fiddling with my tools. As best as I can remember, all brands of vises except one require some amount of adjustment when changing hook sizes. This is not to say that you should avoid those vises—some are among the best on the market—but you should carefully examine the locking mechanisms of the vises in your local fly shop to see if they are relatively simple to use.

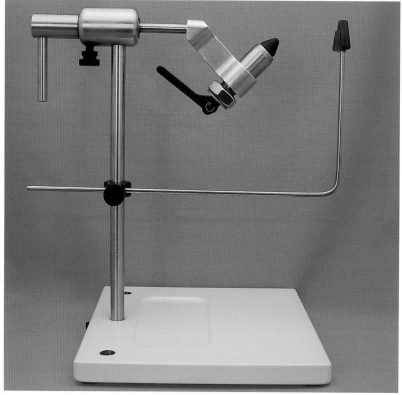
The Peak vise is an example of an affordable rotary vise.

The head on a vise is either stationary or rotates. We will not delve deeply into what is called "rotary" fly tying in this book, but a vise with a rotary head will allow you to easily turn the jaws and hook to examine the fly from all angles. There are excellent vises with stationary heads, but a rotary vise is very convenient to use.

I think the post is one of the most overlooked components of a vise. This steel piece determines the height of the head and jaws from the bench top. This is important because you need ample space to wrap thread and materials on the hook, and very importantly, allow the spool of thread to hang freely from the hook between tying steps; if the thread rests on the tabletop, it will lose tension on the hook and the fly might come apart. Far too many vises, some carrying high price tags, have posts that are too short.

How the vise attaches to the bench top is a matter of personal preference. A clamp, often referred to as a C-clamp, is probably the oldest method. A lot of very experienced tiers prefer vises with C-clamps because these tools grasp the bench top very tightly; tiers who specialize in making deer-hair bass bugs, which requires placing a lot of tension on the thread when fashioning the bodies of these flies, strongly favor C-clamp vises. Also, because the vise post travels through the clamp beyond the edge of the bench, you can adjust the head up or down to raise or lower the jaws. The negative of a C-clamp, especially if you plan to take fly-tying classes or otherwise travel with your vise, is that you must always have a table that can accommodate the clamp on your vise; every experienced fly-tying instructor can tell stories about students who show up for classes with vises that do not fit the tables in the classroom.

A pedestal base is probably the most convenient type of base. These are usually made out of brass or steel, and are typically heavy enough

This Regal vise has a pedestal base.

to hold the vise in place on your bench; I occasionally see aluminum pedestal bases, but these are too light to keep a vise stationary. Although it is more difficult, and sometimes impossible, to adjust the height of the head when using a vise with a pedestal base, you can use this tool anywhere. I prefer using a pedestal base because I often tie flies while sitting in my easy chair and watching a ball game; I just plop the vise on a lapboard and get to work.

I own vises manufactured by several of the leading fly-tying tool companies: Renzetti, Dyna-King, Petijean, and a couple of others. I am using a Regal vise for taking the fly-tying photos in this book. This tool has a pedestal base (although you can purchase it with a C-clamp), and it is the only vise I know of that does not require adjustment when changing hook sizes; simply squeeze a lever to open the jaws, insert the hook, and release the lever. The spring-loaded jaws tightly clamp any hook in place.

So, what's the best way to select a vise? If you belong to a fly-fishing club, ask your fellow members what types and brands of vises they use. Attend a fly-fishing show and see what vises the guest tiers are using; although some will have advanced and expensive tools, others are quite content to use less-expensive entry-level vises. And, of course, visit your local fly shop. Ask for a demonstration of the features and benefits of the vises they have on display. Tell them the types of flies you plan to tie—tiny trout flies, big bass flies, super-size saltwater patterns, or a bit of everything—and inquire which vises will accommodate the range of hooks you will use.

Place a small and then a large hook in each vise you are considering. Which vise does the best job of clamping the hooks in place with a minimum amount of force on the jaw-locking mechanism? Can you easily rotate or swivel the head or jaws to examine the far side while tying? Is the post tall enough so there is ample working space between the hook and tabletop? Can you adjust the height of the post or angle of the head and jaws to increase this working space?

A quality vise will come with a substantial—often a lifetime—warranty. And best of all, you can easily purchase a very high-quality vise—one that will offer a lifetime of fly-tying enjoyment—for $200 or less. Really!

The vise will be the nucleus of your fly-tying station. Select carefully, and you'll have more fun tying flies.

A Good Scissors Is More Than a Set of Sharp Blades

Selecting the correct scissors is one of the least understood aspects of fly tying. A good scissors is more than a set of sharp blades and two holes for your fingers. Quality scissors are actually designed to cut specific materials. For example, there are scissors designed for clipping soft or natural materials such as thread, fine hair, and feathers. There are scissors made for cutting hard materials: wire, tinsel, and synthetic ingredients. And there are scissors designed for clipping thicker hair such as deer hair.

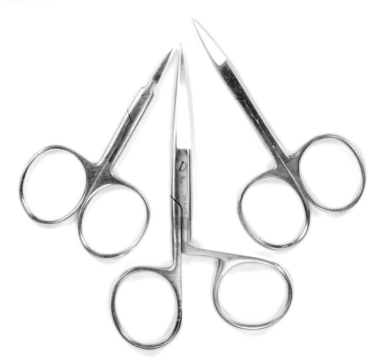

Many fly shops carry the wide Dr. Slick line of fine scissors.

The pegboards of your local fly shop will probably be full of different styles and sizes of scissors, but let's limit today's purchase to two tools. First, you'll want scissors for cutting thread and other soft materials. This delicate implement will have extremely sharp and very pointed blades, and feel lightweight in your hand. These scissors come in different lengths, so if this is your first purchase, choose one with medium-length blades; this middle-of-the-road scissors will work well for almost all applications.

You'll also need a second set of scissors for cutting hard materials. While the blades on these scissors are also sharp and pointed, they are markedly heavier than scissors made for cutting soft ingredients. If you look carefully, you'll notice that the screw or rivet holding the blades together is also beefier; if you chop hard materials using delicate scissors, you'll both dull the fine blades and loosen the lightweight screw that joins the blades together. And finally, one of the blades will have noticeable serrations; these are designed to grip the material while the other, non-serrated blade does most of the actual cutting. (Scissors

Montana Fly Company offers scissors and other tying products in camo coloring.

designed for clipping deer hair, such as when tying deer-hair bass bugs, have even larger serrations for grasping the thick-fibered hair.)

Purchase the best delicate scissors that you can afford; these high-quality scissors will make tying flies easier and more enjoyable. With respect to scissors for cutting tough ingredients, you can buy an expensive tool or save a few dollars and select a less-expensive scissors. I often buy cheap, chrome-plated scissors for cutting wire, tinsel, and similar materials, discarding them when they become dull or the blades loosen; fortunately, it takes tying many, many dozens of flies to destroy even inexpensive scissors.

Later, as you gain experience and begin tying a greater variety of flies, consider adding a scissors for trimming deer-hair bass bugs or the heads on flies such as Muddler Minnows. You might also try new scissors that do not have finger loops, but are designed to lie in the palm of your hand while you continue tying.

GETTING A GRIP WITH HACKLE PLIERS

"Pliers" is such an ugly word when discussing something as beautiful as fine hackle, but the tool used to grasp a feather when wrapping it on the hook is called a hackle pliers. You can also use hackle pliers to grip tinsel and similar materials when wrapping the ribs on flies.

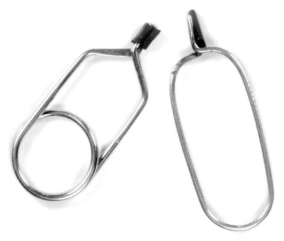

Hackle pliers are inexpensive, essential tools you'll find in any fly shop.

There are different styles of hackle pliers, but the favorite and most common are called English hackle pliers. There is not a lot to say about English hackle pliers: you squeeze the tool together to open the jaws of the pliers, insert the tip of the feather, and release the tension on the tool to close the jaws and grasp the feather. Next, slip your index finger into the hole in the pliers and wrap the feather up the hook. We can, however, say a few things about selecting and adjusting an English hackle pliers.

First, there is no need to spend more than a couple of dollars on hackle pliers; I have collected a fistful of pliers over the years, and I still use my first tool, which cost no more than $2. Occasionally, however, a pliers will snip off the stem of the feather; this can happen even with better-quality pliers. A small burr in the tip of the pliers can nick the stem and cause it to break, or the pliers might have too much tension and crush the stem. You can return the pliers to your fly shop for an exchange, or you can try a couple of simple remedies to fix the problem. If the pliers seem too tight—in other words, you must apply a lot of pressure to open the jaws—squeeze the pliers together to fully open the jaws. This simple step often removes some of the tension in the spring-loaded tool and reduces the chance that the jaws will crush fine hackle stems. If you suspect that one of the jaws has a burr, cover the jaws with small pieces of masking tape, or slip a small piece of narrow-diameter rubber tubing on each jaw. Conversely, if the pliers do a poor job of grasping a hackle, covering the jaws with tape or tubing will eliminate this problem.

Choosing and Adjusting a Bobbin

A bobbin is a small device that holds a spool of thread. It performs at least three functions. First, the bobbin prevents the thread from coming off the spool between tying operations; you can let the bobbin and spool hang from the hook while preparing more materials or taking a break. Second, the weight of the bobbin and spool hanging from the hook maintains thread tension and prevents the fly from unraveling.

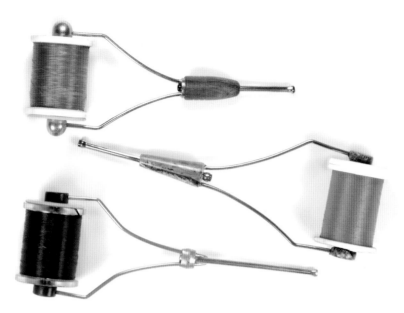

A bobbi will help you maintain proper thread tension when tying a fly.

And third, when tying the fly, you will grasp the bobbin rather than the spool; the thread will remain cleaner, and you will be less likely to fray the thread.

Just like with all of the tools we have discussed so far, there are a variety of different styles of bobbins. If you are new to fly tying, select a simple bobbin found in any fly shop. The two legs of the bobbin hold the spool of thread under tension, and you will slip the end of the thread through the narrow-diameter tube in the bobbin.

Most tiers do not realize it, but the bobbin should be adjusted for the size of thread you are using. Lightly bend the legs of the bobbin out to reduce the tension on a spool of lightweight thread, or bend them together to increase the tension on heavier or stronger thread. Curiously, many professional tiers have strong preferences for how much tension a bobbin places on the spool, and you will develop your own preferences through experience at the vise.

The end of the tube is the most important consideration when selecting a bobbin. Most bobbin tubes are made of brass or aluminum, and the ends will occasionally have microscopic burrs that will nick fine fly-tying thread. Before leaping to the assumption that a poorly manufactured tube is the culprit, try this experiment. Adjust the tension on the bobbin so the thread comes off the spool more easily; some tiers will blame the bobbin tube for breaking thread when excessive tension is the real problem. If the thread continues snapping, return the bobbin to the fly shop for an exchange.

Rather than purchasing a bobbin with a simple metal tube, select what is called a ceramic bobbin. This term is not really accurate because the bobbin is actually not made of ceramic, but the tube has a ceramic insert to prevent nicking or fraying.

If you are an experienced tier and like to experiment with new tools, you might want to try Rite Bobbins. These bobbins are popular with some tiers, but others who are used to grasping standard two-legged bobbins find them difficult to hold. The advantage to the Rite Bobbin is that you can adjust the tension on the spool by just turning a screw.

The end of this ceramic bobbin will protect the thread from fraying.

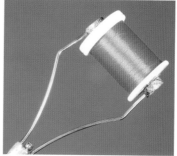

Spread the arms of the bobbin to adjust the tension on the thread spool.

Turn the screw at the end of the Rite Bobbin to adjust the tension on the bobbin.

A Hair Stacker, Whip-Finisher, and Other Doodads

Let's talk about a couple more tools you should add to your fly-tying kit, and a couple that are nice additions but you can live without; you can add these as you gain experience and determine exactly what types of flies you enjoy making.

First, I couldn't live without a hair stacker; if you plan to tie trout flies or bass bugs, you'll also need a stacker. A hair stacker does not actually stack hair; instead, you will use it to even the tips of the hair, typically deer and elk hair. (Occasionally, you might use the stacker to even the butt ends of the hair.) Do you plan to tie flies such as the Elk-hair Caddis? Then you will use the stacker to even the tips of the elk hair before tying the bunch to the top of the hook to create the wing of the fly. Examine the bins of flies in your local fly shop, and you will see scads of patterns tied with similar wings; most of them required a hair stacker.

Hair stackers come in many sizes from very small to very large, and are typically made of brass, aluminum, or even exotic woods. A fellow

There are many sizes and colors of hair stackers.

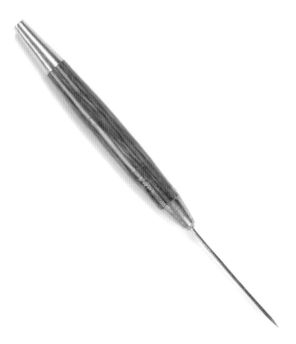

The bodkin is a handy tool.

once gave me a custom-made stacker that measures about 5 inches long and is more than 1 inch in diameter. He said it was designed for evening the tips of bunches of bucktail fibers, but so far it's been more of a curiosity on my fly-tying bench than a practical tool. For tying typical trout flies, select a medium-size stacker measuring about 2 inches long. Flip to the chapter on basic fly-tying techniques to discover how to use this handy little device.

A bodkin is a large needle with a handle used for applying drops of glue to a fly, picking out feather and hair fibers, and a host of other common tasks. You'll definitely need a bodkin. Some bodkins have plain metal handles, but others are made of antler tips, wood, and other materials.

A lot of tiers make the thread heads and final knots that complete their flies using whip-finishers. A whole lot more tiers struggle with

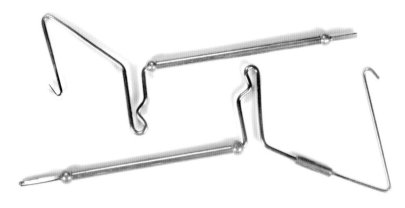

Whip-finish tools

their whip-finishers and find this the most difficult part of making a fly. A whip-finisher, which looks like an instrument of torture, is actually an ingenious fly-tying tool. I will illustrate how to use a whip-finisher in the chapter on fly-tying techniques. I will also show you how I complete a fly: by making three or four half-hitch knots.

I also could not tie flies without single-edge razor blades. These are handy for performing many operations from cutting materials to length to cutting the thread from the final thread knot when completing a fly. I typically use single-edge razor blades more than scissors.

A couple of other simple items will make tying a more pleasurable experience. A saucer, for example, is an ideal place for setting hooks, beads, and similar small ingredients. Leave these items in the saucer until you need them and they'll never get lost in the other items on your desk.

A small foam block is a great place to stick finished flies until you place them in your fly box. I have several different foam devices that slip onto the post of my vise that hold flies, but I find that they sometimes get in my way when tying. I place the foam block anywhere on my bench, and it never interferes with my tying.

A saucer helps organize materials while tying flies.

As you gain experience, you will discover other tools that will help you create better fish-catching flies. For example, if you tie a lot of flies with bead heads, a tweezers designed to grasp fly-tying beads is a handy tool. You can either purchase tweezers that have small indentations for securely gripping beads, or wrap a couple pieces of masking tape around the ends of regular tweezers to help you grab beads.

THE BEST LIGHTING AND THE PROPER WORKSPACE

Too little is written about setting up the proper space for tying flies. Tying flies should be physically relaxing, but poor lighting can lead to eye strain and headaches, and positioning the vise at the wrong height can lead to a sore neck or shoulders. Whether you make a permanent fly-tying station in your home or set up your vise and lay out materials every time you tie, take a few moments to create a good environment.

First, make sure you have ample light to see your work. Tying near a large window that permits lots of natural sunlight to enter the room

A piece of foam is a great place to keep flies while the glue on the heads dry.

is great, but not always possible, especially if you plan to tie in the evening. I prefer using two gooseneck lamps with 75- or 100-watt bulbs that re-create natural daylight. You'll find these inexpensive bulbs at all discount retailers. When tying using regular incandescent or fluorescent bulbs, the light from these bulbs will alter the color of the materials you are using, and the fly will look different in real daylight than it did in your vise. The light emitted from natural-daylight bulbs, however, has less of an impact on the color of materials, so your fly will look remarkably similar whether it is in your vise or on the end of your tippet when fishing.

When setting up your vise, select a bench or table—or raise or lower your chair—so that the jaws are slightly below the height of your chest. If the jaws are too low, and you have to bend your head forward to see your work, you might strain the back of your neck. If the jaws are too high, you will have to raise your arms into an uncomfortable position to tie and thus strain your shoulder muscles.

Place a hook in the vise, and lay a small piece of paper or index card on the table on the other side of the vise. You should see the hook against the paper. The color of the paper should contrast with the color of the fly you are tying; white usually works unless you are tying a white fly. The paper will make it much easier to see your work. You can splurge and purchase an attachment for your vise called a backing plate, which accomplishes the same thing as my 3-cent sheet of paper.

Sure, you can see the fly, yet the tan body and brown hackle get a little lost against the background.

An off-white card placed behind the vise makes the fly much easier to see.

Chapter 2

Basic Fly-Tying Skills

Tying quality, fish-catching flies is not difficult, but you do need to learn some basic procedures. You'll use some of these techniques on all the flies you make, such as starting the thread on the hook and tying off the thread after completing the fly; these sound obvious, but it's surprising how many beginning tiers struggle with these steps. Other tasks, such as using a hair stacker, are important for tying only specific types of patterns; when you wish to make these patterns, some of which are quite common—such as the Elk-hair Caddis—it is essential to know how to manipulate the materials and use the tools.

I suggest practicing the following steps a few times before tying flies. Practice makes perfect, and learning these essential steps comes with repetition. It's similar to a musician practicing the scales; it's not terribly interesting—you might even call it monotonous—but it is essential for learning to make music. For example, we'll start with the very first step: how to start the thread on the hook. It sounds so simple, yet it confounds too many novice tiers. Practice this basic—and mandatory—procedure a few times, and you'll quickly learn how to start the thread. Practice all of the following elementary steps, and you'll learn to tie flies faster and with more confidence.

HOW TO START THE THREAD ON THE HOOK

"Starting the thread" means to tie the thread to the hook shank when beginning a fly. As you will see, we do this without the aid of a knot; we will firmly wrap the thread back on itself against the hook shank. Sometimes you will start the thread near the hook eye and cover the

1. Grasp the end of the thread between your left thumb and forefinger, and the bobbin in your right hand. (These instructions are for a right-handed tier; reverse hands if you're a southpaw. My right hand, which is holding the bobbin, is out of view on the bottom.) Place the thread against the back of the hook shank.

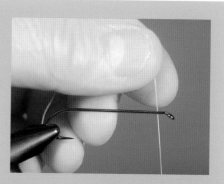

2. Hold the tag end of the thread up and to the left at a 45-degree angle. Make two wraps on the hook shank.

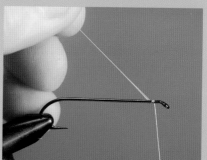

3. Start wrapping the working thread—that's the thread coming out of the bobbin—toward the end of the hook. You're actually wrapping the working thread over the tag end. If you are careful, each new wrap will neatly slide down the angled tag end and slip into place next to the previous wrap.

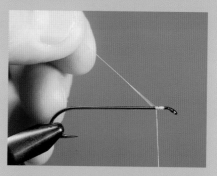

4. Maintain tension on the thread; if you raise the bobbin and lose tension, the wraps will loosen and unravel on the hook. Clip the tag end of thread and continue tying the fly.

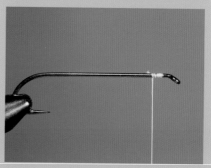

hook shank with a layer of thread, or perhaps tie the wing on a dry fly before making the rest of the pattern. On many flies, however, the tail is the first component you will tie to the fly; in this case, it is faster and more economical to start the thread near the end of the hook shank.

How to Tie Materials to the Hook

Here's another common problem area: tying on materials so as not to create unsightly bumps in a finished fly.

First, securing a material to the hook doesn't require as many wraps as you might imagine. I often see the students in my classes applying half a dozen or more wraps to tie on the first material, and then another half dozen wraps for the second ingredient, and so on; they often pile up all these thread wraps in the same spot on the hook. By the time they're done, they have created a lump of thread about the size of a ping-pong ball!

The fact is that it typically requires only three or four firm wraps of thread to secure a piece of material to the hook. When you tie on the second ingredient, the next set of thread wraps will also help hold the first material in place. It's not a question of *how many* wraps, but making firm wraps in the correct places on the hook.

Whenever possible, taper the butt ends of any thick material you tie to the hook. Tapered ends help create a level underbody, and the completed body will appear smooth with no bumps.

1. On this fly, the first step is to tie on the tail. Therefore, we will start the thread near the end of the hook shank.

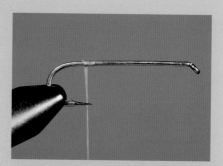

2. The tail on this pattern is made of bucktail. Let's first see how *not* to tie on the tail. First, I measured the bucktail against the hook to determine the length of the tail. Next, I cut off the excess fibers from the butt end of the material, and tied the tail to the top of the hook. The blunt end of the tail will make it impossible to wrap a neat, level body. We can do better than this!

3. Here I have measured the bucktail against the hook to determine the length of the tail. I then tied the bunch to the top of the hook, but I have not clipped the butt ends.

4. Carefully trim the butt ends of the bucktail at an angle; this creates a very gentle transition from the base of the tail to the front of the fly.

5. This fly will have a floss body and tinsel rib. Tie on the floss using only two or three firm thread wraps. The butt end of the floss extends to the front of the hook and becomes part of the underbody. Next, tie on the tinsel using another three or four wraps; it takes no more to hold the tinsel in place.

6. Spiral-wrap the thread up the hook shank. As you can see, the underbody is level.

7. Wrap the floss up the hook to make the body of the fly. Tie off and clip the excess floss. Spiral-wrap the tinsel up the hook to create the rib. Tie off and snip the remaining piece of tinsel. By planning ahead, tying on the materials in the correct manner, and limiting the number of thread wraps, we created a platform for tying a neat body.

Don't Crowd the Hook Eye

Crowding the hook eye and running out of room to complete a pattern is a universal problem for beginning fly tiers; even experienced tiers, if they do not plan ahead when making a fly, have this problem. Fortunately there is a simple solution.

If you start the thread at the front of the hook, leave a small amount of bare wire between the eye and the first thread wrap; you'll eventually tie the head of the fly in this empty space. The first thread wrap closest to the hook eye is like the proverbial line in the sand; you do not want to cross it. You should only cross the last wrap when wrapping the thread head and completing the fly.

If you start the thread near the end of the hook and then work up the shank, leave that same small length of bare wire when you wrap toward the hook eye. Once again, the wrap closest to the eye establishes a line you will not cross until you are ready to complete the pattern.

1. Leave a small amount of bare wire between the hook eye and the first thread wrap. Do not cross this line until you are ready to wrap the thread head and complete the fly.

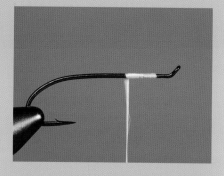

2. Here's our completed fly. The wing, tied using squirrel tail hair, often gives beginning tiers fits; they run out of room and their flies have fat, bulbous heads. We had ample space to complete this pattern, the head is neat and trim, and the wing is tied firmly to the hook.

MEASURING THE PARTS OF A FLY

Since every fly requires a hook, it was only natural that tiers used this as their point of reference when describing the size of the parts of a pattern. For example, you'll see instructions such as "the tail is equal to the length of the hook shank," or "that wing is equal to the overall length of the hook." Hook dimensions, rather than English or metric units, became a convenient shorthand for measuring the parts of a fly. Using the hook as a reference makes it possible to change sizes and create flies of the same relative proportions. Also, tiers can share pattern recipes and, if they are conscientious in their work, create flies that look very similar.

Look at these three hooks. Although they are designed for making different styles of flies—freshwater streamer, saltwater, and salmon/steelhead (*from top to bottom*)—they all share the same components that we can use for measuring the parts of flies: the length of the shank, the width of the gap, the distance between the hook point and the point of the barb, and the length of the overall hook.

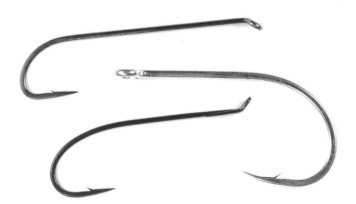

Use the Half-Hitch Knot

The simple half-hitch knot, which you can make using only a flick of your fingers, is one of the most important knots in fly tying. It performs a couple of critical procedures. I use a half-hitch after tying on almost every new part of a fly. I don't know where I picked up this habit, and I didn't even know I did it until a student in a fly-tying class asked what I was doing. But if I break the thread, the fly will unravel only to the last half-hitch; I simply restart the thread on top of the half-hitch and continue tying the fly. Also, if I accidently raise the bobbin and lose tension on the thread, the fly can unravel only to the last half-hitch. Obviously, making a half-hitch on the hook is a good idea if you want to take a break and leave your tying bench; you can be assured that nothing will disturb your work and ruin the partially dressed fly in your absence. And finally, I actually complete the head on a fly and tie off the thread with only three or four half-hitches and a drop of cement; I've been doing this for 40 years, and the heads on my flies never come apart.

Place a hook in your vise and spend some time learning to make the half-hitch knot.

1. Place the thread under moderate tension using your left hand (below the photograph). Place your forefinger and middle finger against the thread.

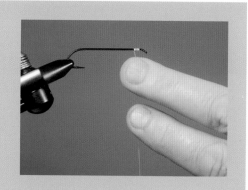

2. Raise the bobbin to the left of the fly and simultaneously flip your hand over; notice that the thread is now crossing next to your forefinger.

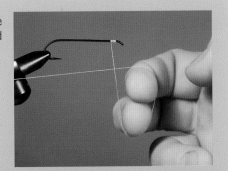

3. Loop the thread onto the hook where you want to place the half-hitch; maintain thread tension while you work.

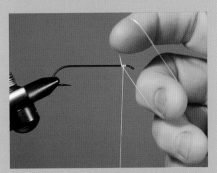

4. Pinch the loop of thread. Pull down on the bobbin to close the loop. Continue pinching the thread to maintain tension and follow the loop to the hook. If you either release the loop or lose thread tension, you will fail to tie the half-hitch. (Read that sentence a second time; it's important.)

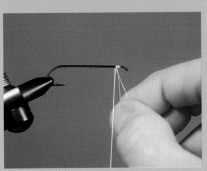

5. Continue pinching the loop of thread all the way to the hook shank. There, our half-hitch is complete. Make this simple knot several times while you tie a fly, and if you snap the thread or lose thread tension, the fly will come apart only to the last half-hitch.

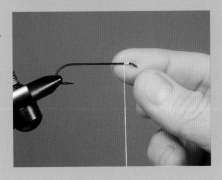

Making the Whip-Finish Knot

A lot of tiers tie off the thread of their flies using the whip-finish knot. While I tie off the thread on all my flies using just a series of simple-to-tie half-hitch knots, I can, when pressed, make a whip-finish knot using both a whip-finishing tool and even just my two fingers. At some point, however, you will be curious and want to know how to use a half-hitch tool. Here's how:

1. The half-hitch tool looks more like an implement of torture than a fly-tying tool. We will use it to make our whip-finish.

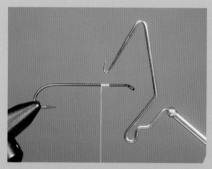

2. First, the thread crosses over the hook in the end of the tool.

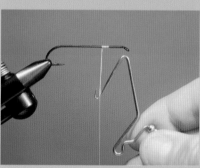

3. Next, the thread crosses over the indentation in the arm near the handle of the tool.

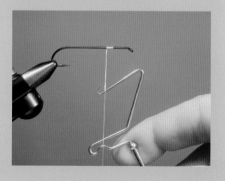

4. Loop the thread behind and to the left of the tool.

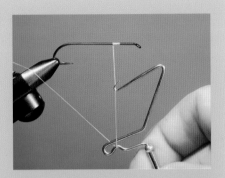

5. Maintain thread tension and flip the tool over. The thread going to the left and leading to the spool and bobbin crosses over the thread coming from the hook, forming the small triangle we see here.

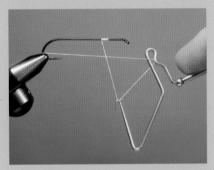

6. Allow the tool to rotate, and raise the tip of the triangle to the hook. The thread coming from the back of the tool is starting to cross over the thread leading to the bobbin; this is the start of the first wrap of the whip-finish.

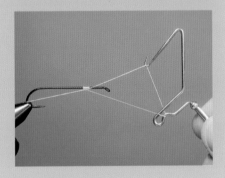

7. Continue rotating the hook at the end of the tool around the hook in the vise; you're wrapping the thread coming from the tool over the thread leading to the bobbin. Make five or six wraps.

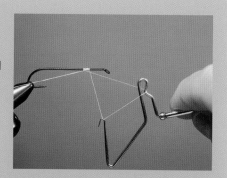

8. We've made the wraps of our whip-finish knot. The hook in the tool should now be above the fly.

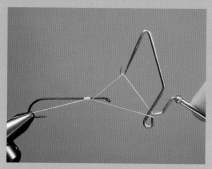

9. Now we'll complete the whip-finish; continue maintaining thread tension as you work. First, raise the hook and lower the back end of the tool to the fly. Release the thread from the bend in the tool.

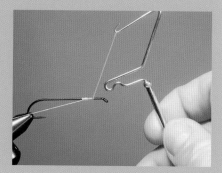

10. Pull the spooled thread to the left (out of the photo), simultaneously lowering the hook to the fly.

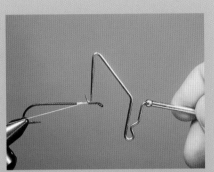

11. Slip the hook out from under the thread. Tighten the knot. We've completed our whip-finish!

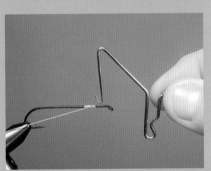

12. I've snipped the thread to prove the strength of our whip-finish. Add a drop of cement, and this knot will remain secure. If you elect to complete your flies using the whip-finish, spend some time practicing this knot.

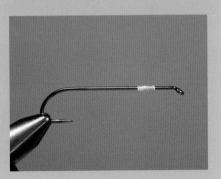

How to Use a Hair Stacker

The hair stacker is an important tool for tying some of the most common dry flies, such as the Elk-hair Caddis. Use the hair stacker to even the tips of the hair used for fashioning the wings on these flies.

Evening the tips is a pretty straightforward affair, but a lot of tiers seem to have problems removing the hair from the tool and tying it to the hook; they remove the bunch in the wrong direction, change hands to place it on the hook, and before they know it, the tips are almost as uneven as before they used the stacker.

Let me show you the proper—and very simple—way of using this common fly-tying tool.

1. Here's a patch of deer hair; I like using this material for making the wings on high-floating caddisfly, stonefly, and similar patterns. It's impossible to tie neat wings with these uneven hairs. I'll use a hair stacker to even the tips of the hair before making the wing.

2. Clip a small bunch of hair from the hide. Brush out the fibrous underfur from the base of the bunch. Place the bunch, tips first, in the hair stacker. Tap the base of the stacker several times on your tying bench; the hairs will fall to the bottom of the closed stacker, evening the tips.

3. Remove the base from the hair stacker; *do not* remove the hair. As you can see, the tips of the hairs are even. At this point, a lot of tiers remove the hair, switch the bunch from hand to hand, and the tips become uneven again. Rather than doing that, simply place the bunch of hair—still in the stacker—on top of the fly. Determine where you wish the tip of the wing to end and proceed to the next step.

4. Grasp the tip of the hair and remove the stacker; do not alter the relative position of the bunch to the fly. Lightly pinch the hairs to the hook.

5. Continue pinching the bunch to the hook, and make four or five firm thread wraps. Tighten the thread.

6. Tie off the thread under the flared hair behind the hook eye. Snip the thread. Clip the excess butt ends of the hair to make the head of the fly. The tips of the hair remained even to create a good-looking wing.

EFFICIENT CUTTING WITH SCISSORS

Sometimes it's challenging to cut a piece of material from the hook without accidently clipping something else. This is especially true after wrapping the thread head and snipping the thread. Rather than using the scissors in the conventional way—both blades cutting the material—try cutting the thread or other ingredients using only one of the sharp blades. Simply grasp the material tight, place the blade against the fly, and slice the material as if you were using a knife.

We've tied the fly and are ready to cut the thread. We want to cut the thread but not accidently clip any of the hackle fibers. First, pull the thread tight. Next, place the sharp scissor blade against the hook. Cut the thread using one firm stroke as if you were using a knife.

Chapter 3

How to Tie
High-Floating Dry Flies

There's nothing quite as thrilling as seeing a wild trout pluck a floating fly from the surface of the water. This is considered the epitome of the sport. For many anglers, fishing with any other type of pattern—wet flies, nymphs, and streamers—is just an activity to pass the time until a hatch of insects begins and the trout start rising. Oftentimes those other patterns catch more trout, and sometimes, especially streamers, consistently catch larger fish, but successfully fishing with dry flies is more fun and memorable.

First, let's define the term dry fly. A *dry fly* is a pattern designed to float on the surface of the water. A great many dry flies are designed to imitate specific forms of trout prey—mayflies, caddisflies, stoneflies, damselflies, and more. Some imitative dry flies mimic specific periods in the life cycles of these insects, such as newly emerged adults, when the insects return to the water to lay eggs, or even when they are dying and lying helpless on the surface. We'll tie examples of these different patterns, and you can select hook sizes and colors of materials to match the insects on your own waters.

As you progress with your fly tying, you'll discover other types of dry flies. For example, there are patterns designed to imitate land-born terrestrial insects such as grasshoppers, crickets, inchworms, and similar trout foods. And there are flies, such as the famous Royal Wulff, that we call attractor patterns. Attractor flies imitate no specific insects yet contain enough important features that fish eagerly try to eat them; these features include such things as the correct size and silhouette, and the dimpling on the surface of the water. Even though attractor dry flies look outlandish in the vise, they look like fish food to the trout.

MATERIAL SELECTION

Tie the majority of your dry flies on 'light-wire hooks specifically designed for floating flies. These hooks reduce the weight of these patterns so they float higher and longer on the surface. Also, since most of these flies are trim and slender, unless the pattern recipe specifies differently, choose size 8/0 (70 denier) tying thread; if you are making very small flies—size 22 and smaller—use even finer thread.

You can use a variety of materials for making the dry-fly bodies. Synthetic dubbing, especially Antron and similar ingredients, is very popular. You can also use some fine natural dubbings such as rabbit and squirrel. Use stripped hackle and stripped peacock herl, wrapped up the hook shank, to make many classic dry-fly patterns. And in recent years, closed-cell foam has become popular for tying dry flies. Foam is unsinkable and very durable, and so gains in popularity every year. I am including a couple foam-bodied flies in the section containing pattern recipes.

Most dry flies are tied using hackle. Many novice and even intermediate-level tiers, however, do not understand what properties make for quality dry-fly hackle. The best dry-fly hackles feature the following attributes:

- Except for the very base and tip of the hackle, the feather contains many stiff fibers of similar length.

- The quill is very slender so that it creates little bulk when the hackle is wrapped around the hook.

- The quill is strong so that it does not snap when wrapped on the hook.

- The hackle should not roll over or twist when wrapped around the hook.

- The majority of dry-fly hackle comes from roosters, specifically the neck area of the roosters. The entire neck skin is called a *dry-fly cape*.

- The smallest feathers, used to tie the smallest flies, are found at the top of the cape; this was actually the head area of the bird. The feathers get progressively larger as you work down the cape. When given a choice, select a cape with the widest range of feather sizes.

- In recent years, hackle producers have introduced *dry-fly saddle hackle*. These very long, slender feathers come from the back of the rooster. They are often economically packaged according to fly size; for example, one package of dry-fly saddle hackle will contain enough feathers to tie 100 size 18 or 16 flies. Note that you can typically tie two or even three flies with each long dry-fly saddle hackle, so the package might not contain 100 feathers.

A great deal of emphasis is placed on selecting capes containing even coloration. For example, the hackles on a brown cape should all be brown, the feathers on a light dun (light gray) cape should all be the same hue, etc. As a result, hackle farmers, when sorting and grading their products, place a higher grade on capes containing uniform coloration. A cape containing slightly mottled or various colors is called a variant, and although the individual hackles on that skin might be ideal for tying flies, that cape is downgraded and sells for less money in the store. As a result, variant capes can be a real bargain and a nice way to save a few dollars when buying hackle. And when you think about it, nothing in nature is really one solid color: it's just possible that the mottled hackles from a variant cape will produce more realistic looking flies!

The tails on many dry flies are made using feather fibers stripped from a dry-fly hackle; typically, the feather for the tailing fibers and the hackle for the collar will all come from the same cape. You can also make the tails on dry flies using synthetic Microfibbetts or Tailing Fibers; these are very similar to the fibers found on fine synthetic artist paintbrushes. And some pattern recipes call for tails tied using very small bunches of Antron yarn; these imitate the empty skins of adult insects just emerging to the surface of the water.

Wings are always a popular area for developing new fly-tying materials. Small hen hackles, slips clipped from duck, goose, and turkey quills, and wood duck and mallard flank feathers have all been used for many decades for fashioning dry-fly wings. Elk and deer hair are also very popular wing materials. High-floating cul de canard feathers, which come from the posteriors of waterfowl, make excellent wings on many dry flies. And there are dozens of flies with wings tied using poly-propylene yarn and a wide assortment of synthetic ingredients.

Because of the popularity of fishing dry flies, tiers have developed literally thousands of floating patterns. We, however, are going to tie just a handful, a standard, classic-style March Brown with the hackle collar wrapped around the hook shank; a Parachute Sulphur with the hackle wrapped around the base of the wing; my version of the Elk-hair Caddis; and, so you have something to match a stonefly hatch, the Stimulator. Once you learn to make these flies, you can switch hook sizes and colors of materials to create your own fish-catching variations. When you begin adding these additional patterns, you've opened the door to tying dozens and dozens of flies that will fool trout.

TYING A MARCH BROWN

Every aspiring fly tier needs to know how to craft classic Catskill-style dry flies. These patterns are fundamental to the art of fly tying and sport of fly fishing. They are characterized by their upright wings, slender bodies, and delicate hackle collars wrapped perpendicular to the hook shanks. These flies generally require few materials, and once you master the tying techniques, you'll be able to create a fly box full of important fish-catching patterns.

We'll use the March Brown as an example of how to tie a classic dry fly. This pattern requires a size 10 hook, which gives ample room to tie the fly.

Hook: Regular dry-fly hook, size 10
Thread: Brown 8/0 (70 denier)
Wing: Wood duck or mallard (dyed lemon yellow) flack feathers
Tail: Ginger hackle fibers
Body: Light brown Antron dubbing
Hackle: Dark ginger and grizzly

1. Tie the March Brown on a size 10 dry-fly hook. This generous-size hook is ideal for learning how to make this classic pattern.

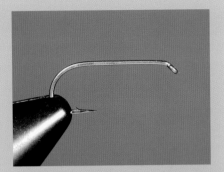

2. Start the thread on the hook. Wrap a thread base for tying on the wings.

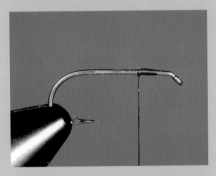

3. Place two wood duck or mallard flank feathers back to back, curving out in opposite directions. Measure the feathers so the finished wings will be about equal to the length of the hook. Pinch the feathers to the top of the hook shank. Tie the feathers to the hook.

4. Clip the excess butt ends from the base of the feathers.

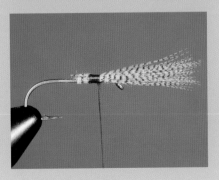

5. Pinch the feathers upright. Wrap a small dam of thread in front of the feathers.

6. Carefully separate the feathers. Make three or four figure-eight wraps between the feathers to establish the two wings.

7. Strip the excess fibers from the base of a brown and a grizzly hackle. Tie the hackles to the hook so the first fibers on the base of the feathers are behind the wings.

8. Clip the tag ends of the hackles. Wrap the thread to the end of the hook. Tie on the tail of the fly. The butt ends of the tail overlap the tag ends of the hackles.

9. Spread dubbing wax on the thread. Spin a sparse pinch of dubbing on the waxed thread. Wrap the dubbing up the hook to create the body of the fly.

10. First, we'll wrap one of the hackles. Make two wraps behind the wings, and two or three wraps in front of the wings. Tie off and snip the surplus hackle tip.

11. Wrap the second hackle; make two wraps behind the wings, and two or three wraps in front of the wings. Tie off and clip the excess piece of hackle.

12. Tie off and cut the thread. Coat the thread head with a small drop of cement.

TYING THE PARACHUTE SULPHUR

A parachute wet has a couple of excellent attributes. First, it rests low on the water and does a fine job of fooling the wariest trout; many times fish, even if they are feeding on the surface, will pass up a standard dry fly but they will eagerly strike its low-riding cousin. The hackle fibers, splaying out from the wing post, create the appearance of legs when viewing the fly from the bottom. And finally, a parachute pattern almost always lands right side up on the water.

A parachute fly is a little more difficult to tie than a classic-style pattern. You'll follow the same techniques for constructing the tail and body, and tying on the wing is a breeze. The challenge comes when wrapping the hackle around the wing post, and then finally tying off and clipping the remaining piece of feather.

I'll show you how to create a dainty Parachute Sulphur on a size 14 hook. Use this method to make even smaller parachute patterns. Fish these flies, and you will catch more trout.

Hook: Regular dry-fly hook, size 14
Thread: White, tan, or yellow 8/0 (70 denier)
Tail: Ginger hackle fibers
Abdomen: Stripped ginger hackle quill
Thorax: Sulphur-colored Antron dubbing
Wing post: Yellow or cream polypropylene yarn
Hackle: Ginger or light grizzly

1. Start the thread on the hook. Strip a small bunch of fibers from a hackle. Tie the fibers to the top of the hook to form the tail of the fly. The tail equals the length of the hook shank. Hint: There's a powerful urge to use a very small number of hackle fibers to match the three tails on a real mayfly, but this will not hold the back end of an artificial on the surface of the water. Using a few more fibers helps create a high-floating dry fly.

2. Tie the butt ends of the tail fibers to the hook; wrap the thread up the shank to create a level underbody.

3. Parachute wing posts are tied using a wide variety of materials; I prefer synthetic polypropylene yarn. Fold a small bunch of yarn under the hook shank. Place the post about one-quarter of the way down the hook.

4. Wrap the thread up and down the base of the wing post. This creates a platform for the hackle.

5. Strip the fibers from the base of a saddle hackle. Tie the bare feather stem to the hook shank. Note that I am placing the feather on the near side of the post; doing this allows the feather to wrap neatly around the post.

6. Strip all the fibers from a saddle hackle. Soak the bare stem in a saucer of water to soften the quill. Tie the slender end of the quill to the base of the tail. Wrap the thread up the hook to where the abdomen will end.

7. Wrap the stripped hackle quill up the hook to create the abdomen of the fly.

8. Tie off and clip the surplus piece of hackle quill. Be sure to allow ample room to make the fly's thorax.

9. Spin a pinch of dubbing on the thread and wrap the thorax. Now we'll wrap the hackle collar. Wrap the feather up the wing post to the top of the thread base. Next, spiral-wrap the hackle down the post to the hook; work carefully and you will not bind down the hackle fibers from the first set of wraps. Brush the hackle fibers up and tie off the excess hackle tip behind the hook eye. Carefully clip the hackle tip.

10. Brush the hackle fibers up, and carefully tie off and snip the thread.

11. Cut the wing post to length. I think you will discover that polypropylene yarn is an ideal, easy-to-use material for tying wing posts.

Tying the Improved Elk-hair Caddis

The Elk-hair Caddis is one of our all-time favorite patterns. It is also one of the first flies taught in tying classes. The reasons are simple: it catches a lot of fish, and it is fairly easy to make. Indeed, even the most experienced angler usually has at least a couple of rows of Elk-hair Caddises in his dry-fly box.

I tie a slight variation of the Elk-hair Caddis with a spring of cul de canard feather under the hair wing. Cul de canard, often referred to as CDC, comes from the rump area of ducks. These small feathers float like corks and add to the buoyancy of any dry fly. I call this simple pattern the Improved Elk-hair Caddis.

Hook: Regular dry-fly hook, sizes 18 to 10
Thread: Size 8/0 (70 denier)
Body: Antron dubbing
Hackle: Dry-fly hackle
Underwing: Cul de canard
Wing: Elk or deer hair

Note: Tie the regular Elk-hair Caddis and my Improved Elk-hair Caddis in a variety of sizes and colors to match the real adult caddisflies you encounter when fishing.

1. Let's turn our attention to the feather we'll spiral-wrap up the body of the fly. First, select a hackle; the fibers should be only slightly longer than the width of the hook gap. Strip the fluff from the base of the feather. Strip a few fibers from the hackle that will lie against the body; this will allow the fibers to splay out nicely when you begin wrapping the hackle up the body.

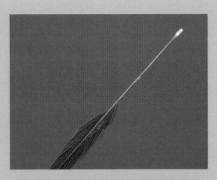

2. Place the hook in the vise. Start the thread and tie the hackle to the end of the hook shank. Note that the little bit of bare stem is facing up. You'll see why this is important later.

3. Spin a pinch of dubbing on the thread.

4. Wrap the dubbing up the hook to form the body of the fly.

5. Spiral-wrap the hackle up the hook. Tie off and clip the excess piece of feather.

6. Clip the fibers on the top of the fly.

7. Strip the fibers from the base of a cul de canard feather. Tie the bare stem to the top of the fly using three light thread wraps.

8. Pull the cul de canard feather to length under the thread wraps. This method maximizes the number of precious CDC fibers on the fly. The CDC underwing extends slightly past the end of the hook.

9. Tighten the thread. Clip the surplus piece of cul de canard. Lock the feather in place with three or four more tight thread wraps.

10. Stack a small bunch of elk hair in a hair stacker to even the tips. Remove the hair from the stacker. Pinch the bunch to the top of the fly. Continue pinching the hair to the fly and make three firm wraps of thread. Help hint: Pinching the hair to the hook while simultaneously wrapping the thread prevents the wing from spinning around the hook under the pressure of the thread.

11. Clip the excess hair to form the stubby head of the fly. Tie off the thread under the head and clip.

Tying the Stimulator

Although the importance of stoneflies and stonefly hatches varies with location, every dry-fly box should have at least a few stonefly imitations. The Stimulator is a great, high-floating pattern that is a favorite among fly fishermen. Start with a larger size; even if you don't encounter real stoneflies of this size on your local waters, it will still make a great searching pattern. As you develop the knack for making the Stimulator, make progressively smaller versions of this fly.

Hook: Straight or curved long-shank dry-fly hook, sizes 16 to 12
Thread: Size 6/0 (140 denier)
Tail: Deer or elk hair
Body: Tan Antron dubbing
Wing: Deer or elk hair
Hackles: Grizzly dyed tan or light brown

1. Although you may use a dry-fly hook with an extra-long straight shank, the Stimulator is typically made on a hook with a slightly curved shank.

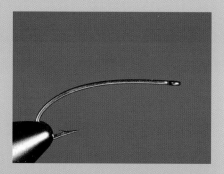

2. Start the thread on the hook. Wrap a thread base on the last two-thirds of the shank. Leave the thread hanging at the front end of the thread base.

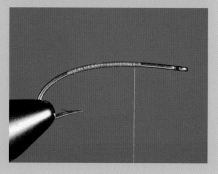

3. First we'll tie the tail of the fly. On the Stimulator, start making the tail on the front of the thread base. Clip a narrow bunch of deer hair from the hide. Clean the underfur from the base of the bunch. Tie the hair to the top of the hook with the tips pointing toward the end of the fly.

4. Here's the deer hair tied to the top of the hook. The tips of the hair extend slightly beyond the end of the hook shank.

5. Pull the hair toward the end of the hook. Spiral-wrap the thread to the end of the hook, binding down the deer hair along the shank. Firmly tie down the deer hair at the end of the shank.

6. Tie on a piece of wire at the base of the tail.

7. Smear dubbing wax on the thread. Spin a pinch of dubbing on the waxed thread.

8. Wrap the dubbing up the hook to create the abdomen of the Stimulator.

9. Strip the fibers from the base of a dry-fly hackle. Tie on the hackle in front of the abdomen; use firm thread wraps to secure the feather to the hook.

10. Spiral-wrap the hackle down the hook to the tail of the fly. Most tiers make this hackle thick to increase the buoyancy of the Stimulator.

11. Maintain tension on the hackle. Spiral-wrap the wire up the hook over the wrapped feather. Now you may release the feather from the hackle pliers; the wire locks the feather to the fly. Tie off the excess wire.

12. Clip the surplus piece of wire. Here we see the first half of the Stimulator. Leave at least one-third of the front end of the hook shank to accommodate the thorax and wing.

13. Clip a bunch of deer or elk hair from the hide. Comb the underfur from the bunch of hair. Even the tips in a hair stacker. Tie the bunch to the top of the hook to make the wing of the fly. Note that the tips of the wing extend to the tips of the tail.

14. Clip the butt ends of the wing at an angle.

15. Cover the butt ends of the wing with firm thread wraps.

16. Strip the fluffy and excess fibers from the base of a dry-fly hackle. Tie on the hackle at the base of the wing.

17. Smear dubbing wax on the thread. Spin a pinch of dubbing on the waxed thread. Wrap the thorax of the fly.

18. Wrap the hackle over the thorax. The hackle collar is full and bushy. Tie off the surplus hackle tip.

19. Clip the hackle tip. Wrap a neat thread head, whip-finish, and snip.

TYING THE QUIGLEY CRIPPLE

It happens a couple of times when I write a magazine article, and it occurs several times when writing a book: I start discussing some little gem of information to which I hope you pay a little closer attention. I think everything in the article or book will help you become a better tier or angler, but these tidbits deserve special attention. These are the things that can take your tying and fishing to a whole new level.

Tying and fishing emerger imitations is one of these subjects. Fish emergers at the proper times and you *will* catch more trout.

In its most generic sense, an *emerger* is the stage of development in the life of an aquatic insect between the larval and adult stages. Most anglers key into fishing either larval or adult imitations, while the fish often key into feeding on emergers. Why do so many of us miss this important stage of insect development and overlook this important opportunity to catch fish?

The Quigley Cripple is a terrific imitation of an adult insect—probably a mayfly—that has failed at emerging and turning into a fully formed adult. It's sort of halfway between being an emerger and an imitation of an adult, but we fish it as a dry fly.

Hook: 2X-long wet-fly hook, sizes 16 to 12
Thread: Size 6/0 (140 denier)
Trailing shuck: Cream or tan Antron
Abdomen: Turkey or goose biot, or Antron dubbing
Thorax: Rabbit dubbing
Wing: Deer or elk hair
Hackle: Dry-fly hackle

Note: Popular colors for the Quigley Cripple are brown, tan, light olive, medium olive, and dun.

1. Start the thread on the middle of the hook. Tie on a small bunch of Antron fibers.

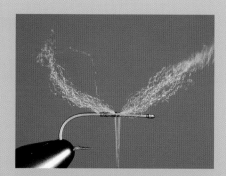

2. Fold the Antron back, and wrap the thread to the end of the hook.

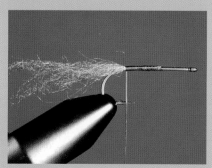

3. Clip the Antron to length—usually equal to or slightly less than the length of the hook shank.

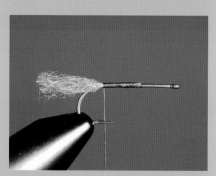

4. Tie on the tip of a goose or turkey biot. The curved side of the biot should face the hook. Neatly wrap the thread up the hook to the point where the abdomen of the fly will end.

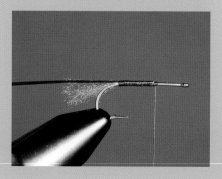

5. Wrap the biot up the hook to make the abdomen. Tying on the biot with the curved side facing the hook creates the nice body segmentation.

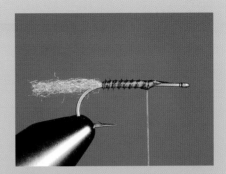

6. Smear dubbing wax on the thread. Spin a small pinch of rabbit or similar dubbing on the waxed thread. Wrap the dubbing on the hook to create a slightly shaggy abdomen; be careful, however, not to use too much dubbing.

7. Clip a small bunch of deer hair from the hide. Clean out the underfur from the base of the bunch. Even the tips of the bunch in a hair stacker. Next, remove the hair from the stacker and place it on the top of the hook with the tips pointing forward. Pinch the hair to the top of the hook and make four or five firm thread wraps. A half-hitch holds the hair in place.

8. Clip the butt ends of the deer hair. Leave a small tab of hair behind the thread wraps to help define the thorax of the fly and add buoyancy to the pattern.

9. Select a dry-fly hackle. Strip the excess fibers from the base of the feather. Clip the bare quill if necessary, and tie the hackle to the side of the fly.

10. Wrap a full hackle collar behind the deer-hair wing. Tie off and clip the surplus hackle tip.

11. Wrap a neat thread head. Whip-finish and snip the thread. When fishing, the Antron trailing shuck and biot abdomen will sink slightly below the surface of the water, and the hackle and deer-hair wing will float above the surface.

Bomber

Hook: 2X-long dry-fly hook, size 10 or 8
Thread: Size 6/0 (140 denier), color to match the body
Tail: Deer hair
Body: Rabbit dubbing
Hackle: Dry-fly hackle spiral-wrapped up the body
Wing: Deer hair

Note: Fran Betters, a legend in New York's Adirondack Mountains, tied this pattern. Although all of his patterns were scruffy, they all caught fish. Tie the Bomber in white, tan, brown, and rusty orange.

Fan-wing Green Drake

Hook: Regular dry-fly hook, sizes 12 to 8
Thread: Brown 6/0 (140 denier)
Tail: Black hackle fibers
Body: Olive dry-fly dubbing
Rib: Black tying thread
Wings: Gray hen hackles clipped to shape
Hackle: Gray

Note: Hen hackle wings are easy to make and give a fly a sense of realism.

Blue-wing Olive
Hook: Regular dry-fly hook, size 18 or 16
Thread: Olive 8/0 (70 denier)
Tail: Dark gray hackle fibers
Body: Olive dry-fly dubbing
Wings: Gray hackle tips
Hackle: Gray

Sulphur
Hook: Regular dry-fly hook, size 16 or 14
Thread: Yellow 8/0 (70 denier)
Tail: Light gray hackle fibers
Body: Yellow or sulfur-colored dry-fly dubbing
Wings: Light gray hackle fibers
Hackle: Light gray

Fan-wing Coachman
Hook: 2X-long dry-fly hook, sizes 16 to 12
Thread: Brown 8/0 (70 denier)
Tail: Golden pheasant tippet fibers
Body: Peacock herl and red floss
Wings: Slips clipped from white duck shoulder feathers
Hackle: Brown

Royal Humpy

Hook: 2X-long dry-fly hook, sizes 16 to 12
Thread: Red 6/0 (140 denier)
Tail: Moose hair or black hackle fibers
Body: Red floss
Back: Deer or elk hair
Wings: White goat hair
Hackle: Ginger or brown

Note: The red floss in the body denotes this pattern as the Royal Humpy, but you can use any color you wish.

Olive Compara-dun

Hook: Regular dry-fly hook, sizes 18 to 12
Thread: Olive 8/0 (70 denier)
Tail: Light dun hackle fibers
Body: Olive dry-fly dubbing
Wing: Deer hair

Note: Al Caucci and Bob Nastasi developed the Compara-dun style of dry fly in the 1970s. These flies, with fan-shaped deer-hair wings, sit low in the water. Change hook size and colors of materials to create Compara-dun imitations of almost any mayfly.

Griffith's Gnat

Hook: Regular dry-fly hook, sizes 22 to 18

Thread: Black 8/0 (70 denier)

Body: Peacock herl

Hackle: Grizzly

Note: Every angler needs a selection of midge imitations. The simple Griffith's Gnat is easy to tie and catches a lot of trout.

Parachute Adams

Hook: Regular dry-fly hook, sizes 16 to 12

Thread: Gray 8/0 (70 denier)

Tail: Gray dry-fly dubbing

Wing: Fine white goat hair

Hackle: Grizzly and brown

Quill Gordon

Hook: Regular dry-fly hook, size 10
Thread: Brown 8/0 (70 denier)
Tail: Gray hackle fibers
Body: Stripped peacock herl
Wing: Wood-duck flank fibers
Hackle: Gray

Note: The Quill Gordon is one of the most famous patterns in the history of fly fishing. Stripped peacock herl, which is used to make the body of the pattern, is a piece of herl with the short green fibers removed. To remove the fibers, draw the herl between your thumbnail and index finger, or hold the herl securely on your tying bench and remove the fibers using a pencil eraser. Another option is to substitute another material for the stripped herl; a stripped hackle quill or even fine dry-fly dubbing are good options.

Green Renegade

Hook: Standard dry-fly hook, sizes 22 to 4
Thread: Green 6/0 (70 denier)
Tag: Green tying thread
Body: Peacock herl
Back hackle: Brown
Front hackle: White

Baby Boy Hopper

Hook: Regular dry-fly hook, size 10
Thread: Chartreuse 3/0 Monocord
Body: Chartreuse foam
Legs: Chartreuse round rubber legs
Wing: Deer hair

Murray's Little Black Stonefly

Hook: Regular dry-fly hook, sizes 20 to 14
Thread: Black 6/0 (140 denier)
Body: Black dubbing
Hackle: Black
Wing: Black goose biots with clipped tips

Missing Link Caddis

Hook: Regular dry-fly hook, sizes 18 to 12
Thread: Camel 8/0 (70 denier)
Abdomen: Tying thread coated with Softex
Rib: Pearl Flashabou
Thorax/wing splitter: Peacock Ice Dub
Wing: Elk body hair
Hackle: Dark dun dry-fly hackle

Brown Drake Profile Spinner

Hook: Regular dry-fly hook, size 12

Thread: Brown 8/0 (70 denier)

Tail: Brown grizzly stripped hackle stems

Extended abdomen: Larva Lace Dry Fly Foam, yellow, folded over a needle and colored with waterproof marking pens

Rib: Same as the tying thread

Wing post: Orange and yellow macramé yarn

Down wings: Dun Z-Lon

Thorax: Select Buggy Nymph Dubbing, amber caddis

Parachute hackle: Dark dun saddle dry-fly hackle

TCO's Tan Adult Caddis

Hook: Curved-shank emerger hook, sizes 18 to12

Abdomen: Yellow tan TCO's East Coast Dubbing

Thorax: Gray caddis TCO's East Coast Dubbing

Wing: Medium dun cul de canard

Chapter 4

Making Fish-Catching Nymphs and Wet Flies

Even though casting dry flies to rising trout is more exciting, you will usually catch more fish using subsurface patterns such as nymphs and wet flies. Why? Because even though we might get swept away by the thrill of seeing trout feeding on the surface of the water, the fish spend the majority of their time foraging under the surface, usually near or at the streambed.

Want more proof of the importance of fishing nymphs and wet flies? In recent years, what are called European nymph-fishing tactics have become all the rage. Contestants to the World Fly Fishing Championships developed these methods. In a nutshell, anglers use extra-long rods and leaders, and maintain constant contact with their weighted patterns while they fish the runs and lies of streams and rivers. They basically draw the flies downstream and tighten the line if they detect the slightest bump or pause in the presentation. These methods work, and anglers chock large numbers of caught fish.

The anglers and teams who catch the largest number of fish win the World Fly Fishing Championships, and many of them swear by these nymph-fishing techniques. Curiously, I have heard of no new dry-fly fishing methods coming out of the World Championships; the fish spend most of their time feeding on nymphs and larvae, so these contestants spend most of their time fishing subsurface imitations.

In this section we will tie three basic styles of flies. An imitation of an immature mayfly, stonefly, damselfly, and a few other insects are generally called *nymphs*. A larva is an immature caddisfly. And from a fish's point of view, a *wet fly* probably imitates an immature insect swimming or floating to the surface to emerge as a winged adult. We could delve deeper into these definitions and discuss a wide variety of subclassifications of patterns, but those basic descriptions will serve us well; you could use those terms in any fly shop, and the staff and fellow anglers will know what types of flies you are discussing.

MATERIAL SELECTION

Since nymphs, larvae, and wet flies are designed to sink, we use hooks made of heavier wire. These hooks also come with straight shanks as well as curved shanks to give the bodies of the flies a natural-looking bent shape, much like an insect that has been dislodged from the streambed.

You may wrap lead wire or a nontoxic substitute around the hook shank to add weight to a pattern before tying the fly, but over the past 20 years, we've seen an explosion in the number of patterns featuring bead heads. Beads come in copper, tungsten, and other metals. While a bead adds weight to a fly, many anglers swear that the little glint of flash coming off the metal makes a pattern more attractive to the trout.

For tying the bodies of the following patterns, we will use peacock herl, a wide variety of natural and synthetic dubbing, pheasant tail fibers, wire, and other ingredients. Hen hackle is great for making tails and sparse hackle collars. And on some flies, a piece of Flashabou or Flashback adds an important dash of sparkle.

The Copper John—
The Most Popular Fly in the World

Umpqua Feather Merchants, the company that sells the commercially tied Copper John, reports that this is its most popular pattern. And when they toss in the wide variety of color variations—other than copper—as well as similar flies sporting long rubber legs and other parts that they sell, then the entire Copper John family swamps sales of any other pattern. This sounds like a pretty strong recommendation. The Copper John is a pattern you will want to learn to tie.

Copper John

Hook: Curved-shank scud hook, sizes 18 to 14
Head: A small or medium gold or copper bead
Thread: Brown 6/0 (140 denier)
Tail: Brown goose or turkey biots
Abdomen: Medium copper wire
Thorax: Peacock herl
Wing case: Gold Flashabou or Mylar tinsel, and a strip clipped from a turkey tail feather
Legs: Brown mottled soft hackle fibers

1. Consider the lowly fly-tying bead; it's a little more complicated than you might think. After selecting the correct size bead for the fly, you have to know which side faces the hook eye and which side faces the body of the fly. The side of the bead with a small hole drilled through the metal, like the one in the photo, will face the eye.

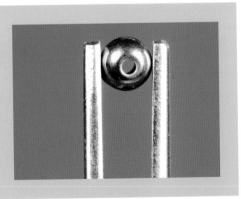

2. The hole on this side of the bead is countersunk. This is the side that will face the body of the Copper John.

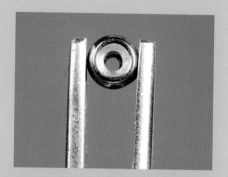

3. Slip the bead on the hook so the small hole faces the eye. Place the hook in the vise. I find it easier to tie a fly on a curved shank with the hook pointing slightly down.

4. Start the thread on the hook. Wrap a layer of thread on the last half of the shank.

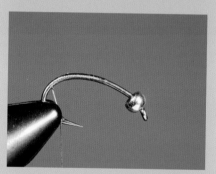

5. Tie the tail using two brown biots. Biots are the short, stiff fibers from the leading edges of goose or turkey wing feathers. Clip two biots from the stem.

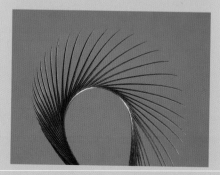

6. Place the biots together so they curve out in opposite directions. Tie the biots to the end of the hook using two or three loose wraps of thread. Right now the biots are a bit too long for the tail of the fly; we'll fix this in the next step.

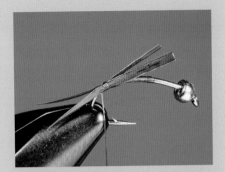

7. Gently pull the butt ends of the biots to shorten the tail to the desired length. Tighten the thread to lock the biots in place and clip the excess. Next, tie a piece of copper wire to the hook. Note that the tag end of the wire extends up the entire hook shank; this creates a level underbody.

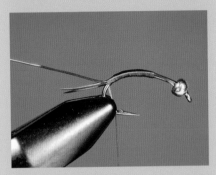

8. Wrap the wire up the hook to make the abdomen of the fly. Tie off and clip the surplus wire.

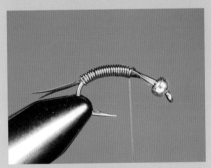

9. Tie a piece of Flashabou or Mylar tinsel to the top of the fly.

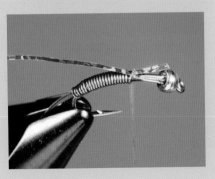

10. Tie a narrow strip clipped from a turkey tail feather to the top of the hook.

11. Tie on several pieces of peacock herl in front of the abdomen. Wrap the thread to the bead.

12. Wrap the peacock herl up the hook to create the thorax of the Copper John. Tie off and snip the excess herl.

13. Tie a small bunch of soft hackle fibers to the near side of the fly.

14. Tie a second bunch of hackle fibers to the far side of the fly.

15. Carefully clip the butt ends of the hackle fibers. Most of the Copper Johns you'll find in fly shops have short legs, but I prefer longer, more robust appendages.

16. Fold the strip of turkey over the top of the fly to form the wing case. Tie off and clip the surplus piece of feather.

17. Fold the Flashabou over the top of the wing case. Tie off and cut the excess.

18. Tie off and snip the thread. Coat the wing case with epoxy.

19. Here we see the Copper John from the side. It's fairly easy to see why the trout mistake this pattern for a small stonefly nymph.

Tie a Basic Wet Fly: The Peacock Bead-head

A good fish-catching fly doesn't have to be complicated; oftentimes the simplest pattern is also the best. It must, however, have certain features that fool a fish into thinking it is something good to eat. The Peacock Bead-head requires only a couple of materials: a bead head to make the fly sink, a basic peacock-herl body to create the silhouette of an insect, and a sparse hen-hackle collar that imitates the kicking legs of an emerging insect. The Peacock Bead-head is very simple and, at times, very deadly.

Peacock Bead-head

Hook: Regular wet-fly hook, sizes 16 to 12
Thread: Brown 6/0 (140 denier)
Body: Peacock herl
Hackle: Wet-fly soft hackle

1. Slip the bead on the hook; the countersunk hole in the bead faces the fly body.

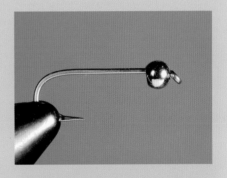

2. Start the thread on the hook. Leave a long tag of thread hanging out the end of the hook shank.

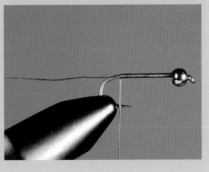

3. Tie on several pieces of peacock herl; the tag ends of the herl extend the length of the shank to create a level underbody.

4. Twist the thread and the peacock herl together.

5. Wrap the thread and herl up the hook to create the body of the fly.

6. Tie off the body of the fly. Snip the remaining thread and herl.

7. Select a hen hackle. Strip the fluffy fibers, which we see here, from the base of the feather.

8. Tie the bare hackle stem to the fly; the good side of the feather should be facing forward or up.

9. Wrap the hackle twice around the hook. Tie off and clip the surplus feather tip. Whip-finish the thread behind the bead and snip.

A Classic Wet Fly That Still Works Well

I feel strongly that far too many anglers do not respect the fish-catching potential of basic, old-fashioned wet flies. When tied properly—that means *sparsely*—they usually have more fish-attracting power than the most intricately tied nymphs. A slender body, meager tail, and wispy hackle for legs convince trout that a wet fly is an emerging insect and something good to eat. Tie up this generic wet fly in the colors of your choice, and use it on your local waters. I know you will be pleased with the results.

Classic Wet Fly

Hook: Regular wet-fly hook, sizes 16 to 12
Thread: Brown 6/0 (140 denier)
Tail: Hackle fibers
Abdomen: Flat tinsel
Thorax: Rabbit dubbing
Hackle: Hen hackle

Note: Select materials in colors of your choice.

1. Strip the fluffy fibers from the base of a hackle. Start the thread on the hook. Tie the hook to the top of the shank with the good side of the feather facing away from you.

2. Wrap the thread to the end of the hook shank. Tie on a small bunch of hackle fibers for the tail of the fly.

3. Tie a piece of flat silver to the hook. Wrap the thread up the shank to where the abdomen will end.

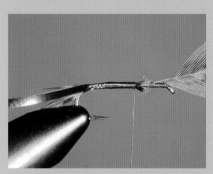

4. Wrap the tinsel up the hook to create the abdomen. Tie off and clip the surplus piece of tinsel.

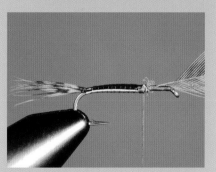

5. Spin a very small pinch of dubbing on the thread. Wrap the dubbing on the hook to create the thorax.

6. Wrap the hackle twice around the hook. Tie off and snip the excess hackle tip.

7. Brush the hackle fibers back. Wrap a neat thread head; wrap the thread to the base of the hackle to hold the fibers back. Tie off and snip the thread.

Big Dave's Caddis Emerger: One of My Own

I have never, ever named a pattern after myself. So this time, just for the hell of it, I decided to finally do just that. Oh, I'll never call it Big Dave's Caddis Emerger in public, but just this one time, let me have some fun.

This pattern will require you to stretch and challenge your skills. It's a fine imitation of an emerging caddisfly, which is commonly called a pupa. Sometimes the trout are locked into feeding on caddisfly pupa, and you will catch many more fish if you have an appropriate matching pattern. The head, legs, and antennae create excellent movement in the water.

Follow the instructions, work slowly, and be patient. In the end, you will have a fly that *will* catch fish.

Big Dave's Caddis Emerger

Hook: Regular wet-fly hook, sizes 12 to 8
Thread: Brown 6/0 (140 denier)
Abdomen: Nymph Skin or a similar material colored with a permanent marker
Rib: Brown 3/0 (210 denier) thread
Thorax: Hare "E" Ice Dub or squirrel dubbing
Legs and antennae: English partridge or coq de Leon hackle
Head: Pheasant aftershaft feather

1. Start the thread on the hook shank. Clip the end of a piece of Nymph Skin or a similar material at an angle. Tie the tip of the Nymph Skin where the front of the abdomen will end.

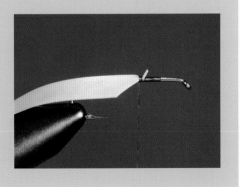

2. Lightly stretch the Nymph Skin and wrap the thread down the hook shank. Tie on a piece of 3/0 (210 denier) tying thread. Wrap the working thread back up the shank.

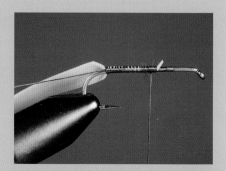

3. Stretch the Nymph Skin and start wrapping the abdomen. Reduce the tension on the Nymph Skin to wrap a progressively wider body and create a tapered abdomen. Tie off and clip the excess Nymph Skin.

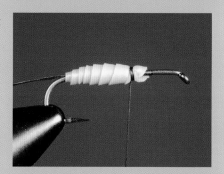

4. Wrap the 3/0 thread over the abdomen to create the rib. Tie off and clip the excess thread. This piece of thread accentuates the segmentation on the finished fly.

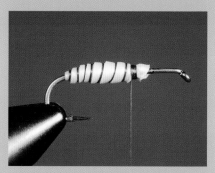

5. Color the abdomen using a brown permanent marker. (You may omit this step if you use a material of the desired final color.) Nymph Skin is a latex product, so I seal it with a drop of head cement.

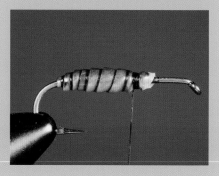

6. Insert a pinch of dubbing between the fibers of the thread. Spin the bobbin to lock the dubbing in the thread.

7. Wrap the dubbing on the hook to create the beginning of the abdomen.

8. Strip the fibers from the base of a soft hackle. Tie the bare stem of the hackle to the hook with the feather hanging over the hook eye.

9. Make two wraps of hackle. Tie off and clip the excess piece of feather. Next, brush the hackle toward the end of the fly. Wrap the thread over the base of the hackle fibers.

10. Snap the weak tip from a filoplume feather. Strip some fibers from the base of the feather. Tie the bare stem to the hook in front of the hackle fibers.

11. Wrap the filoplume up the hook to complete the thorax. You might need to brush the fine fibers back as you wrap the feather. Tie off and cut the excess piece of filoplume.

12. Tie off and snip the thread. Carefully place a drop of cement on the thread knot; don't let the glue get on the fine filoplume fibers.

Making Large Fish-Catching Nymphs

For as long as I can remember, fly anglers have admired large, well-tied imitations of golden stonefly and other large nymphs. We love the patterns, and we dream about the rivers where the real insects live. Indeed, from the East Coast to the West Coast, and from our southern trout waters all the way into Canada and Alaska, you can find a host of medium- to monstrous-size stoneflies.

If you fish moving water for trout, you will need a selection of stonefly nymphs. Here we will make my large Golden Stonefly Nymph, but you can swap colors of materials to create patterns that imitate brown or black stoneflies. If you wish to make smaller patterns, omit the hen-hackle legs and simply pick out the thorax dubbing to imitate the legs of the real insects.

Like with many of the flies in this book, you are free to substitute materials. I am using Nymph Skin for the abdomen, but you may select Scud Back or one of the many similar products you will find in your local fly shop. Other than Nymph Skin, which doesn't have wide distribution in the United States (although it is available), you should easily find all of the ingredients listed in the pattern recipe in your neighborhood fly-tying emporium.

Golden Stonefly Nymph
Hook: Partridge Czech Nymph Hook or your choice of curved-shank nymph hook, sizes 14 to 10
Bead: Gold bead, size to match the hook size
Thread: Brown 6/0 (140 denier)
Antennae and tail: Brown goose or turkey biots
Abdomen: Nymph Skin or a similar material colored with permanent marker
Thorax: Golden yellow Hare "E" Ice Dub or angora dubbing
Legs: English partridge or a coq de Leon hen hackle
Wing case: Brown Medallion Sheeting or a similar material

1. Slip a gold bead onto the hook shank. Place the hook in the vise.

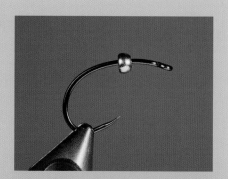

2. Slip the bead to the back end of the hook. Start the thread behind the hook eye. Tie on two turkey or goose biots to create the antennae. Tie off and snip the thread. Coat the thread wraps with cement.

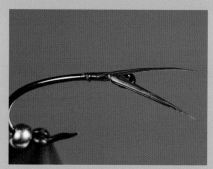

3. Slip the bead over the thread wraps.

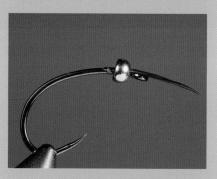

4. Restart the thread directly behind the bead.

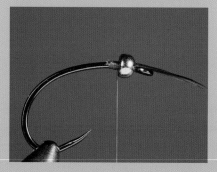

5. Cut a piece of lead wire equal to the length of the body of the fly. Cut one end of the wire at an angle. Place the blunt end of the wire against the back of the bead, and tie the wire to the side of the hook. Note that the back end of the wire angles down to the hook; this will make it easier to wrap the body material.

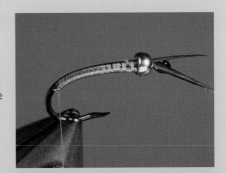

6. Cut a second piece of lead wire. Tie the wire to the other side of the hook shank.

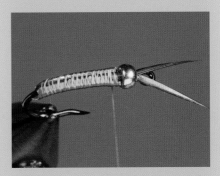

7. Here we're examining our work from the side of the hook. The wire, tied to the sides of the hook, adds weight and creates a broad but narrow underbody.

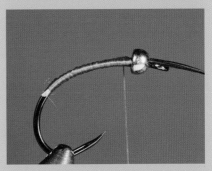

8. Coating the thread wraps with cement locks the wire to the sides of the hook shank.

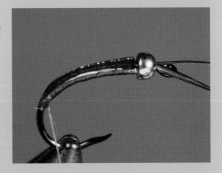

9. Clip the end of a piece of Nymph Skin, Scud Back, or a similar material at an angle. Tie the narrow tip of the material to the end of the hook. Wrap the thread up the hook.

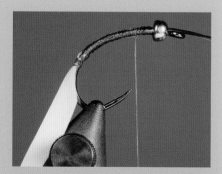

10. Pull the Nymph Skin tight. Make two or three wraps of Nymph Skin to create the butt end of the abdomen. Hold a biot on the near side of the hook. Make one wrap of Nymph Skin over the biot.

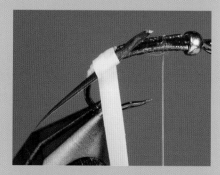

11. Hold a second biot on the far side of the hook. Continue wrapping the Nymph Skin up the hook; the body material holds the biot tails in place. Gradually reduce tension on the Nymph Skin to create progressively wider body segments. Tie off the Nymph Skin and examine the fly. If you're not pleased with the appearance of your work, simply unwrap the thread and body material, and wrap the abdomen again.

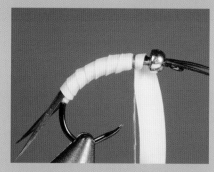

12. Stretch and clip the surplus body material.

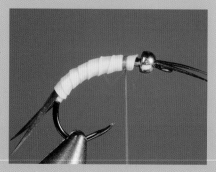

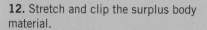

13. Wrap the thread down the hook to where you will begin making the thorax of the fly.

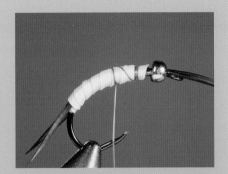

14. You may wish to color the top of the abdomen with a brown permanent marker.

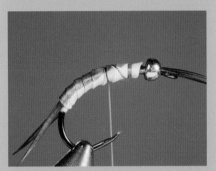

15. Here we're examining the top of the fly. Beyond admiring my artwork, I want you to compare this photo to the previous step. Note that the abdomen has a natural, wide silhouette.

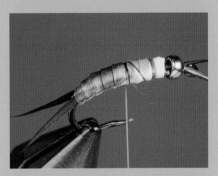

16. I am using Nymph Skin, which is a latex product. Coat the abdomen with cement to seal the material from the air.

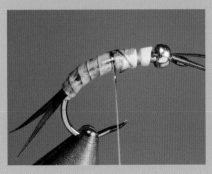

17. Check out the side of the pattern. The cement causes the permanent marker to run down the sides of the body and become slightly mottled, giving the abdomen a more realistic appearance.

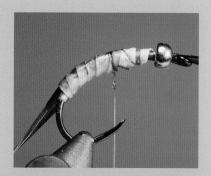

18. Clip a piece of Medallion Sheeting or turkey tail feather equal to the width of the wing case. Tie the material to the top of the fly.

19. Before making the dubbed thorax, we have to prepare the hen feather for fashioning the legs of the fly. Strip the fluffy fibers from the base of a mottled colored feather. Next, gently brush out the fibers that will become the legs; the stem, from the base of the fibers to the base of the intact tip, approximately equals the length of the thorax we will tie. I'm making a large Golden Stonefly Nymph, so I'll prepare two feathers; one feather is sufficient when making a smaller pattern.

20. Stack the feathers. Tie the feathers to the hook in front of the abdomen; place the thread wraps at the base of the intact tips.

21. Tighten the thread wraps. Clip the excess feather tips.

22. Make a dubbing loop. Smear a very small amount of dubbing on the loop. Spread dubbing in the loop, and twist the loop closed.

23. Wrap the dubbing up the hook to create the thorax. Tie off and cut the dubbing loop.

24. I prefer pulling the hen feathers forward over the top of the thorax one at a time. Pull the first feather forward and tie down with one firm wrap of thread.

25. Pull the second feather forward and secure with one firm thread wrap.

26. Clip the bases of the feathers, temporarily leaving a small amount of the stems.

27. Pull the Medallion Sheeting over the top of the hook to make the wing case.

28. Make several firm thread wraps. Cut the surplus pieces of Medallion Sheeting and feather stems.

29. Whip-finish the thread and clip. Coat the thread wraps with cement. Our completed Golden Stonefly Nymph looks pretty good!

30. Here's a side view of our Golden Stonefly Nymph.

Poxy Back Nymph

Hook: 3X-long nymph hook, sizes 14 to 10
Thread: Tan 6/0 (140 denier)
Head: Gold bead, size to match the hook
Tail: Goose or turkey biots
Abdomen: A goose or turkey biot
Thorax: Dubbing
Legs: Hen hackle under the wing case
Wing case: A slip of turkey tail feather covered with a drop of epoxy

Psycho Prince

Hook: Regular nymph hook, sizes 18 to 12
Thread: Tan 8/0 (70 denier)
Tail: Brown turkey biots
Abdomen: Ice Dub
Rib: Copper wire
Carapace: Golden brown turkey tail
Wing tuft: Angel Hair
Wing: Turkey biots
Collar: Arizona Synthetic Peacock Dubbing

Note: Tie this pattern using a variety of colors of materials.

Root Canal

Hook: Regular wet-fly hook, size 16

Head: Copper bead

Thread: Brown 6/0 (140 denier)

Tail: Gray hackle fibers

Abdomen: Brown tying thread

Rib: Fine copper wire

Thorax: Dark gray squirrel dubbing

Hot spot: Hot red tying thread

Cased Caddis Larva

Hook: 4X-long nymph hook, size 12

Thread: Chartreuse 3/0 (210 denier)

Head: Black bead

Body: Pheasant tail fibers wrapped on the hook and coated with head cement

Head: Chartreuse Hare "E" Ice Dub

Note: This simple pattern is an imitation of a cased caddis larva. It is one of the best patterns I know for catching trout in streams and rivers.

Big Black Stonefly

Hook: 3X-long nymph hook,
sizes 12 to 6
Thread: Black 6/0
(140 denier)
Head: Gold bead
Tail: Turkey biots
Body: Black dubbing
Wing case: Slips clipped from
a dark turkey feather or a substitute
Legs: Rubber legs
Antennae: Turkey biots

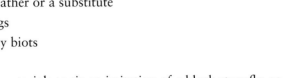

Note: Use black materials to tie an imitation of a black stonefly, or
light tan ingredients to make an imitation of a golden stonefly.

Damselfly Nymph

Hook: 4X-long nymph hook,
sizes 14 to 10
Thread: Olive 6/0 (140 denier)
Tail: Olive hackle fibers
Abdomen: Narrow olive
Stretch Tubing
Thorax: Olive squirrel dubbing
Wing case: Turkey tail feather
Legs: Brown hen hackle fibers
Weight: Micro dumbbell eyes

Note: Bending the hook as shown helps the fly ride in the correct
position in the water.

Torrey's Favorite

Hook: Curved-shank nymph hook, sizes 18 to 12

Thread: Brown 6/0 (140 denier)

Head: Black tungsten bead

Abdomen: Brown dubbing

Rib: Narrow pearl Krystal Flash

Hot spot: Orange dubbing

Back: Clear Thin Skin or a narrow strip clipped from a freezer bag

Flashback Pheasant-tail Nymph

Hook: Regular nymph hook, sizes 18 to 14

Thread: Black 8/0 (70 denier)

Tail, abdomen, thorax, and legs: Pheasant tail fibers

Rib: Gold wire

Wing case: Narrow Flashback tinsel or Flashabou

West Grand Bead-head Wet Fly

Hook: Regular wet-fly hook, size 14
Head: Gold bead
Thread: Brown 6/0 (140 denier)
Tail: Tan hen hackle fibers
Abdomen: Medium brown Stretch Tubing
Thorax: Brown rabbit or squirrel dubbing
Hackle: Brown hen hackle

Note: I tie this pattern for fishing the Hendrickson hatch at Grand Lake Stream, Maine, the first couple of weeks of May. Try this pattern wherever you encounter these important mayflies.

Euro Nymph

Hook: Curved-shank nymph hook, sizes 16 to 12
Thread: Brown 6/0 (140 denier)
Head: Black tungsten bead
Abdomen: Gold floss covered with clear D-Rib or Stretch Tubing
Hot spot: Orange floss
Thorax: Peacock Ice Dubbing
Wing case: Clear Thin Skin or a strip clipped from a freezer bag

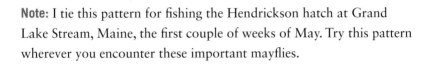

Note: Over the past decade, nymphs and larvae featuring brightly colored hot spots have become all the rage. These flies, although they resemble nothing in nature, do catch trout.

Bead-head Marabou
Royal Coachman

Hook: 2X-long wet-fly hook,
size 14 or 12

Thread: Red 6/0 (140 denier)

Head: Gold bead

Tail: Golden pheasant tippet
fibers

Body: Peacock herl and red
floss or tying thread

Wing: White marabou

Hackle: Tan brown hen hackle

Note: Okay, I'm going to turn you on to a tip that might make
reading this entire book worthwhile: The Bead-head Marabou Royal
Coachman is my number-one pattern for catching brook trout.
Actually, with or without the bead, and whether I'm fishing ponds or
streams, this unlikely fly slays the fish. We spend so much time trying
to craft realistic-looking patterns that sometimes it's attractor flies that
catch the trout.

Hovering Damselfly Nymph

Hook: 3X-long nymph hook, size 14

Thread: Olive 6/0 (140 denier)

Tail: Chartreuse rabbit fur or marabou

Abdomen: A thin strip of 1-millimeter-thick closed-cell foam wrapped up the hook shank

Thorax: Peacock herl

Legs: Tan mottled hen hackle fibers

Wing case: Olive closed-cell foam

Eyes: Round chartreuse closed-cell foam

Note: Rather than using a heavily weighted pattern to fish deep, try this buoyant pattern with a fast-sinking line and short leader. The line will draw the fly to the bottom, and the Hovering Damselfly Nymph will hover above the weed line.

Mr. Rapidan Bead-head Nymph

Hook: Regular nymph hook, size 14 or 12

Thread: Brown 6/0 (140 denier)

Tail: Brown hackle fibers

Body: Gray rabbit dubbing

Legs: Brown hackle fibers

Wing case: A mallard flank feather clipped short

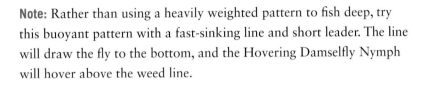

Simply Black Stonefly

Hook: 2X-long nymph hook, sizes 16 to 12

Thread: Black 6/0 (140 denier)

Tail: Black turkey biots

Abdomen: Black dubbing

Rib: Black Stretch Tubing or D-Rib

Thorax: Black rabbit squirrel dubbing

Legs: Black hackle fibers

Wing case: Black goose feather

Flashback Mayfly Nymph

Hook: Regular nymph hook, sizes 18 to 14

Thread: Brown 6/0 (140 denier)

Head: Gold bead

Tail: Pheasant tail fibers

Abdomen: Pheasant tail fibers

Rib: Gold wire

Thorax: Tan rabbit dubbing

Wing case: A strip of turkey tail feather and a piece of Flashback or narrow Flashabou coated with epoxy

Starling and Purple

Hook: Regular wet-fly hook, sizes 20 to 12

Thread: Purple 8/0 (70 denier)

Abdomen: Tying thread

Thorax: Peacock herl

Hackle: Starling

CDC Spider

Hook: Short-shank wet-fly hook, nymph hook, sizes 17 to 13

Thread: Tan 8/0 (70 denier)

Abdomen: Orange/pink scud and shrimp SLF Dubbing

Thorax: Peacock-colored dubbing

Hackle: Dun cul de canard

Mink Nymph

Hook: 2x-long nymph hook, your choice of sizes

Thread: Brown 8/0 (70 denier)

Tail: Three moose body hairs

Abdomen: Amber Super Fine dubbing

Rib: Gray ostrich herl

Thorax: Mink dubbing

Wing case: Turkey

Caddis Emerger

Hook: Curveed-shank emerged hook, your choice of sizes
Thread: Tan 8/0 (70 denier)
Body: Olive/yellow dubbing
Rib: Brown Pseudo Hackle
Wing: Brown elk hair
Antennae: Elk hair
Head: Black Ice Dub

Two-tone Worm

Hook: Cured shank nymph hook, sizes 16 to 10
Thread: Brown 8/0 (70 denier)
Body: Worm brown and wine Micro Chenille
Collar: Datum Glo Brite #5

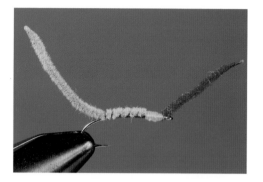

Yellow Miracle Stonefly Nymph

Hook: 2x-long nymph hook, sizes 16 to 12
Thread: Yellow 6/0 (140 denier)
Tail: Yellow biots
Abdomen: Yellow dubbing
Rib: Gold wire
Thorax: Yellow dubbing
Wing case: Yellow quill
Legs: Mottled Indian hen fibers

Charlie's Mysis Shrimp

Hook: Tiemco TMC9300, size 18
Thread: White 8/0 (70 denier)
Abdomen: White Egg Yarn
Thorax: White Egg Yarn cut and mixed into dubbing
Eyes: Small black round rubber legs

Pisco's Caddis Pupa

Hook: Tiemco TMC2499 SP-BL, size 12
Thread: Dark brown 6/0 (140 denier)
Body: Dark olive SLF Squirrel Dubbing
Rib: Extra-small copper Ultra Wire
Underwing: Medium dun cul de canard
Overwing: Natural deer hair
Collar: Dark brown SLF Squirrel Dubbing
Eyes: Melted monofilament

CDC Caddis Pupa

Hook: Tiemco TMC2499 SP-BL, sizes 18 to 12
Bead: Black tungsten or brass
Thread: Brown 6/0 (140 denier)
Abdomen: Chartreuse Ice Dub
Thorax: Peacock Ice Dub
Overwing: Pheasant tail fibers

William's Biot Nymph

Hook: Knapek Nymph Hook,
size 14
Bead: Gold tungsten
Thread: Dark brown 6/0
(140 denier)
Tail: Brown partridge
Abdomen: Mahogany brown
turkey quill
Thorax: Dark brown SLF Squirrel Dubbing
Collar: Dark brown cul de canard
Rib: 5X monofilament

Best Baetis

Hook: Tiemco TMC100 or
equivalent, sizes 22 to 16
Thread: Olive 8/0 (70 denier)
Tails: Brown Z-Lon
Abdomen: Stripped peacock
herl dyed olive
Wing: Medium dun rabbit's
foot fur
Thorax: BWO Super Fine dubbing

Ice Wing RS 2

Hook: Tiemco TMC3769 or
equivalent, sizes 22 to 16
Thread: Olive 8/0 (70 denier)
Tails: Medium dun
Microfibbets
Body: BWO Super Fine
dubbing
Wing: Pearl Ice Dubbing

Chapter 5

Streamers for Catching Big Fish

Big fish eat little fish, and if you want to catch larger trout, you'll want to carry a selection of streamers

A *streamer* is an imitation of a baitfish. Baitfish include minnows, dace, sculpins, and even immature trout; hey, feeding fish don't distinguish between common forage and members of their own tribe.

There is also a group of streamers called attractor patterns. These flies have the streamlined appearance of baitfish, but their colors look like nothing you'll find in nature. Trout strike attractor streamers out of a sense of curiosity, territoriality, or some other fishy instinct. Regardless of why fish attack attractor flies, these patterns do catch fish.

Streamers are ideal for learning how to tie flies. They are larger than other forms of patterns, and provide an excellent platform for learning the basic techniques.

BASIC MATERIALS FOR TYING FISH-CATCHING STREAMERS

Tie streamers on hooks with extra-long shanks; these provide the platforms for tying the bodies for these flies. You can also set aside the extra-light thread, and use 6/0 and even 3/0 thread.

We tie streamers using a wide variety of natural and synthetic materials; covering them all is well beyond the scope of this book. I have selected flies that require only a few of the most basic and affordable ingredients, and you can use some of the materials to tie more than one pattern. The flies are fun to tie, they teach the basic tying skills, and they do catch trout. Our limited palate of materials will include bucktail, hackles, and marabou, as well as tinsel and a couple of common flash materials you will find in any fly shop.

Making the Marabou Brown Trout

Marabou is one of the most important fly-tying materials. Marabou is very soft and gives flies a lifelike, swimming action in the water. It comes in a rainbow of colors, so once you learn the basics of tying a pattern, you can substitute colors to create an almost limitless number of variations. The Marabou Brown Trout is a good example of one of these simple, effective patterns.

Marabou Brown Trout

Hook: 4X- to 6X-long streamer hook, sizes 10 to 2
Thread: Black 6/0 (140 denier)
Body: Gold braided or flat tinsel
Underwing: Yellow and red bucktail
Wing: Tan or light brown marabou, and gold or holographic gold Flashabou

1. Start the thread on the hook. Tie on a piece of braided tinsel. The tag end of the tinsel extends up the hook shank to create a level underbody.

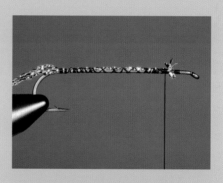

2. Wrap the tinsel up the hook to make the body of the fly. Tie off and cut the extra tinsel.

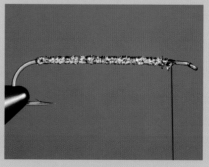

3. Tie a small bunch of olive bucktail to the hook.

4. Tie a small bunch of red bucktail to the top of the fly.

5. Clip the butt ends of the bucktail to create a neat underwing.

6. Strip the excess fibers from the base of a marabou feather. Tie the feather flat on top of the fly using gentle thread wraps.

7. Pull the marabou to length (to the right) to form the wing.

8. Tighten the thread to lock the marabou to the top of the hook. Clip the butt end of the feather.

9. Fold a couple of pieces of Flashabou over the thread. Tie the marabou to the top of the fly.

10. Whip-finish and snip the thread. Coat the thread head with cement.

The Clouser Minnow Catches Trout, Too

Bob Clouser, of Pennsylvania, rocked the fly-fishing world when he tied a small lead dumbbell on top of a hook shank and created what we call the Clouser Minnow. The dumbbell causes the hook to flip over and ride with the point on top so the fly does not snag the streambed. And the weight, placed near the front of the hook eye, gives the pattern a great jigging action. While the Clouser Minnow is widely used for catching bass and a wide variety of saltwater species, the heavy dumbbells make most versions of this fly difficult to cast with trout-size tackle.

Wapsi Fly, the company that created fly-tying dumbbells, does offer small dumbbells ideal for tying lighter-weight Clouser Minnows. I am tying this Clouser Minnow using a dumbbell that weighs a mere 1/80 of an ounce. While the fly is much lighter than most other versions, it still carries enough weight to cause the hook to flip over in the water. You can also easily cast this pattern with a 6-weight rod and weight-forward fly line.

Now, when it comes to trout fishing, you can have your Clouser Minnow and fish it, too.

Clouser Minnow

Hook: 4X-long streamer hook, size 6
Thread: White 3/0 (210 denier)
Eyes: 1/80-ounce dumbbell
Body: Tinsel or tinsel braid
Belly and back: Bucktail
Flash material: Krystal Flash

1. Start the thread on the hook. Tie on a piece of braided tinsel.

2. Wrap the tinsel up the hook to make the body of the fly. Tie off and cut the remaining piece of tinsel.

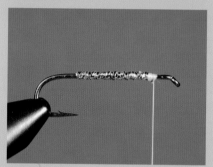

3. Wrap a thread base on the hook for the dumbbell. Tie the dumbbell to the top of the hook using very firm figure-eight wraps. Make two or three firm wraps between the base of the dumbbell and the hook shank to tighten the figure-eight wraps. A drop of superglue welds the dumbbell to the hook.

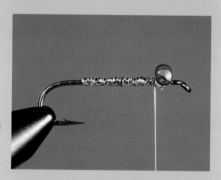

4. Tie on a small bunch of white bucktail in front of the dumbbell. Wrap the thread behind the dumbbell and tie the bucktail down behind the eyes.

5. Clip the butt ends of the bucktail.

6. Flip the hook over in the vise; this is how the fly will ride in the water. Tie a small bunch of bucktail to the top of the hook.

7. Fold a couple pieces of Krystal Flash over the thread. Tie the Krystal Flash to the top of the wing.

8. Tie off and clip the thread. Coat the thread head with cement.

THE THUNDER CREEK

Keith Fulsher developed the Thunder Creek series of streamers in the 1960s and 1970s. His patterns, which imitate almost all the most popular forms of baitfish, are the streamer angler's answer to "match the hatch." What's particularly nice about these flies is that they require very few materials—mostly bucktail. We're going to tie a version that is a close imitation of a brook trout—or so I think—but it catches trophy trout everywhere.

Flip to the pages containing photos of flies and recipes for other patterns to see a Thunder Creek that Keith tied. With their painted eyes, his patterns always have a swept-back, racy look; the heads on my flies are a little larger because I use flashy adhesive eyes. However you make them, the Thunder Creek is a lot of fun to tie and fish.

Black-nose Dace Thunder Creek

Hook: Straight-eye streamer hook, sizes 10 to 4
Thread: White 6/0 (140 denier)
Body: Flat tinsel on the hook shank, and bucktail with strands of black Krystal Flash in your choice of colors
Eyes and gills: Holographic adhesive eyes

1. Start the thread on the hook. Tie on a piece of tinsel.

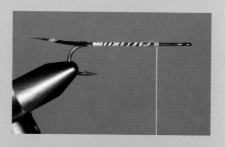

2. Wrap the tinsel up the hook to create the body of the fly. Tie off and cut the surplus tinsel.

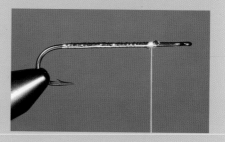

3. Fold two pieces of Krystal Flash or Flashabou around the thread. Tie the flash material to the top of the hook.

4. Tie small bunches of bucktail to the top of the hook; I am using two colors of bucktail to enhance the final color of the fly.

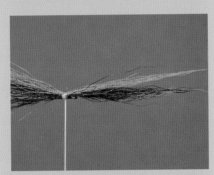

5. Tie a bunch of bucktail to the bottom of the hook.

6. Clip the butt ends of the bucktail. The thread is hanging where the back of the head will end.

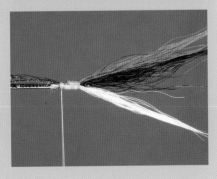

7. Fold the top bucktail back over the top of the hook. Pinch the bucktail back to create a small head. Make three firm wraps to hold the bucktail in place.

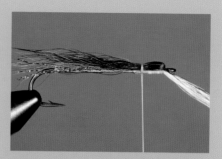

8. Fold the bottom bucktail under the hook. Pinch the bucktail back, and make three firm thread wraps.

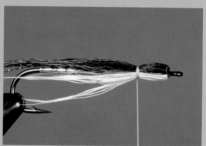

9. Tie off and snip the thread.

10. Cover the head of the fly with a thin coat of epoxy.

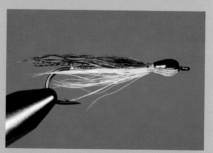

11. You can paint eyes on the flies, but I use extra-small adhesive eyes. Apply another thin coat of epoxy to seal and protect the eyes.

A New Take on Fishing Still Waters:
The Hovering Leech

The vast majority of the literature devoted to fly fishing for trout centers around moving water—rivers, streams, and brooks. This is largely due to two factors. First, there are more opportunities to fish for trout in moving waters as opposed to lakes and ponds. Think about it: Today, even in sections of the South where trout are not native, vast tailwater systems have been developed into prime trout fisheries. Yes, we all mourn the loss of trout habitat due to development, but tailwaters have created thousands of new miles of trout rivers.

Second, fishing a trout pond or lake is hard work and very challenging. It's generally easy to spot potential holding water and good lies in a river or stream; with a little instruction, even a novice can quickly spot the locations that most likely hold fish. By comparison, fishing a pond or lake seems like casting into a deep, dark hole. Where are the trout?

Many subsurface flies designed for fishing trout ponds are packed with weight to make them sink. This sounds like a logical idea: Use a heavy fly to get down to the fish quickly. The problem, however, is that this sort of pattern sinks and sinks . . . and sinks—right to the bottom. It's not long before you've snagged weeds or even more solid objects.

Over the past few seasons, I've employed a new method for fishing trout ponds: I use buoyant patterns with a full fast-sinking fly line. I tether one of these flies to the end of the line using a short leader. The line sinks quickly and draws the fly down with it. Eventually, the line lays on the bottom of the pond while the fly hovers above the weed line. By using a pattern such as my Hovering Leech, I spend more time prospecting for trout and less time cleaning debris off the hook, and I rarely lose a fly.

Hovering Leech

Hook: 4X-long streamer hook, sizes 12 to 8

Thread: Size 6/0 (140 denier)

Underbody: Closed-cell foam

Tail: Marabou and Krystal Flash

Body: Angora dubbing or a synthetic substitute

Note: This pattern works well tied in black, purple, and olive.

1. Start the thread on the hook. Tie the end of a narrow piece of closed-cell foam to the front of the hook shank.

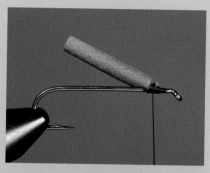

2. Tie down the foam at the end of the hook shank. Make a series of light figure-eight wraps over the foam.

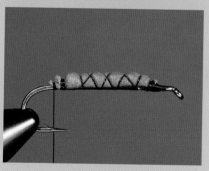

3. Tie a small bunch of marabou to the end of the hook to form the tail of the fly.

4. Fold a piece of Krystal Flash on the thread. Tie the folded material onto the side of the tail. Fold and tie a second piece of Krystal Flash on the other side of the tail.

5. Make a dubbing loop. Spread dubbing in the loop. Spin the loop closed.

6. Wrap the dubbing up the hook. Brush the dubbing fibers back while you work. Tie off and clip the excess dubbing loop. Wrap a neat thread head, whip-finish, and snip. This humble fly is a real fish catcher!

Crystal Bugger

Hook: 4X-long streamer hook, sizes 8 to 4
Thread: Black 6/0 (140 denier)
Head: Gold bead
Tail: Black marabou and green Krystal Chenille
Body: Olive Crystal Chenille, hackle, and rubber legs

Black-nose Dace Thunder Creek

Hook: Straight-eye streamer hook, sizes 10 to 4
Thread: White 6/0 (140 denier)
Body: Brown, black, and white bucktail, with strands of black Krystal Flash
Eyes and gills: Enamel paint

Note: This is a genuine Thunder Creek tied by the originator, Keith Fulsher.

EZY Crayfish

Hook: 6X-long streamer hook, sizes 8 to 4

Thread: Brown 6/0 (140 denier)

Weight: Non-lead wire

Eyes: Bead-chain or dumbbell eyes

Claws: Rusty orange marabou

Body: Rusty brown chenille

Rib: Copper wire

Shellback: Brown polypropylene yarn

Hackle: Brown saddle hackle

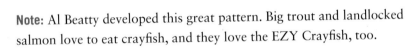

Note: Al Beatty developed this great pattern. Big trout and landlocked salmon love to eat crayfish, and they love the EZY Crayfish, too.

Ritt Sculpin

Hook: 4X-long streamer hook, sizes 8 to 4

Thread: Olive 3/0 (210 denier)

Body: Shaggy olive dubbing

Back: Olive rabbit Zonker strip

Rib: Gold wire

Head: Fish-Skull by Flymen Fishing Company

Note: Flymen Fishing Company is a leading manufacturer of fly-tying beads and other products designed to add weight to flies. The Fish-Skull, which slips on the hook like a bead, is a great way to add weight and realism to a streamer.

Black Ghost

Hook: 6X-long streamer hook,
sizes 8 to 2
Thread: Black 6/0 (140 denier)
Tail: Yellow hackle fibers
Body: Black floss
Rib: Silver tinsel
Throat: Yellow hackle fibers
Wing: White hackle
Eyes: Enamel paint

Note: This is a classic pattern that still catches fish. The eyes are optional, and you can substitute white (or any other color) for the wing.

Ballou Special

Hook: 6X-long streamer hook,
sizes 6 to 2
Thread: Black 6/0 (140 denier)
Tail: A golden pheasant crest
feather curving down
Body: Flat silver tinsel
Underwing: Red bucktail
Wing: White bucktail with
peacock herl on top
Cheeks: Jungle cock

Note: This is another classic pattern. Feel free to drop the tail and cheeks. This is a time-honored fly that catches a lot of trout.

Bead-head Peacock Bugger

Hook: Standard 3X-long streamer, sizes 18 to 2

Head: Copper bead

Thread: Black 6/0 (70 denier)

Tail: Black marabou and copper Krystal Flash

Body: Peacock herl

Rib: Copper wire

Hackle: Black

Mini Zonker

Hook: Standard 3X-long streamer hook, sizes 14 to 6

Thread: Green 6/0 (70 denier)

Tail: Green marabou or yarn

Body: Brown chenille

Rib: Copper wire

Wing: Dark brown Mini Zonker Strip anchored Matuka-style

Hackle: Brown

About the Author

David Klausmeyer is the editor of *Fly Tyer* magazine. His many books include *The Master's Fly Box* and *Rocky Mountain Trout Flies: A Postcard Book* (both by the Lyons Press) and *Tying Classic Freshwater Streamers, Orvis Guide to Beginning Fly Tying, Trout Streams of Northern New England, Striped Bass Flies* and *Better Flies Faster*. David's articles and photography have appeared in *American Angler, Fly Fisherman,* and *Fly Rod & Reel* magazines. In 2006, the Catskill Fly Fishing Center and Museum presented David with the Golden Hook Award for his efforts to promote fly fishing and tying.